DANCing
to the Heartbeat
of Redemption

The Creative Process
of Spiritual Growth

Joy Sawyer

InterVarsity Press
Downers Grove, Illinois

InterVarsity Press
P.O. Box 1400, Downers Grove, IL 60515
World Wide Web: www.ivpress.com
E-mail: mail@ivpress.com

InterVarsity Press® is the book-publishing division of InterVarsity Christian Fellowship/USA®, a student movement active on campus at hundreds of universities, colleges and schools of nursing in the United States of America, and a member movement of the International Fellowship of Evangelical Students. For information about local and regional activities, write Public Relations Dept., InterVarsity Christian Fellowship/USA, 6400 Schroeder Rd., P.O. Box 7895, Madison, WI 53707-7895.

All Scripture quotations, unless otherwise indicated, are taken from the Holy Bible, New Revised Standard Version®. NRSV®. Copyright © 1989 by the Division of Christian Education of the National Council of the Churches of Christ in the United States of America. All rights reserved.

Scripture quotations marked NIV are taken from the Holy Bible, New International Version®. NIV®. Copyright © 1973, 1978, 1984 by International Bible Society. Used by permission of Zondervan Publishing House. All rights reserved.

Cover photograph: Larry Prosor/SuperStock

ISBN 0-8308-2229-1

Printed in the United States of America ∞

Library of Congress Cataloging-in-Publication Data

Sawyer, Joy.
 Dancing to the heartbeat of redemption: the creative process of spiritual growth/Joy Sawyer
  p. cm.
 Includes bibliographical references.
 ISBN 0-8308-2229-1 (pbk.: alk. paper)
  1. Christian poetry, American—History and criticism. 2. Christian poetry,
English—History and criticism. 3. Christian poetry—Authorship. 4. Spiritual formation. 5.
Christian poetry. 6. Creative writing. I. Title.
PS310.R4 S29 2000
811.009'3823—dc21

                                                                    99-053608

20 19 18 17 16 15 14 13 12 11 10 9 8 7 6 5 4 3 2 1

16 15 14 13 12 11 10 09 08 07 06 05 04 03 02 01 00

For Scotty

CONTENTS

Acknowledgments

9

Featured Poets

11

1 Living by Poetry

The Creative Process of Spiritual Growth

15

2 Dancing to the Heartbeat of Redemption

Poetry & Faith

28

3 Conformed to the Image of Love

God in a Red Wheelbarrow

42

4 When Our Soul Sings the Blues

The Jazz Rhythm of Hope

58

5 Developing the Poetic Voice

Shaped by Prayer & Contemplation

75

---

6 Community as Soul Critics

The Poetry Workshop of the Church

87

---

7 The Blessing of Brokenness

"Our Common, Puddled Substance"

109

---

8 Living as Sacred Symbols

Poetry & the Prophetic

123

---

9 Enjoying Beauty's Tension

The Paradox of Pleasure

144

Notes

159

Acknowledgments

Books are community adventures—and this one is no exception. I am forever indebted to a number of people who traveled with me on this journey, sometimes through rocky soul terrain.

First, I'm thankful to a group of mentors, colleagues and fellow writers (in some cases, all three labels apply to the same person) who read and commented on portions or all of this manuscript: Lydia Dean, David DeBoard, Cindy Schott Hunter, Kristy Johnson, Jo Kadlecek, Stephanie Link, Anton Marco, Judith McCune, David Noller, Patricia Sawyer, Scott Sawyer, Mary Shoaff.

I'm also very grateful for the writing mentors I've had throughout the years: Sue Crider Atkins, Sandy Vekasy, Shirley Shedd, Doug Tarpley, Marilyn Quigley, Frances Bixler, Lorie Hartman, William Packard, Galway Kinnell, to name a few. A very special thanks to my mentor of twenty-two years, Anton Marco, for not only his passionate editorial input but also his steadfast love and care.

My years spent in the master's program in biblical counseling at Colorado Christian University were especially memorable and life-changing. Special thanks to Dr. Don Hudson, who first encouraged me to pursue this idea of "the poetry of the soul."

In addition, many thanks to:

My Faith-Drenched Poetry Group, for a lively exchange of poetry and the sacred;

Dr. Donald Capps and Dr. Terry Lindvall, for helpful reading suggestions;

Inklings and the *Mars Hill Review,* for graciously allowing me to explore these ideas in writing;

IVP editors Cynthia Bunch-Hotaling and David Zimmerman for their belief in and guidance of this project, as well as Ruth Goring's thoughtful, creative suggestions;

Our parents, Leon and Barbara Roulier, and Robert and Patricia Sawyer, for their love and prayers.

I'm especially thankful for some very dear friends who gave both their hearts—and hands—when they were needed most: Greg and Lydia Dean (remember the shepherd's pie and the "Texas chili"?); Karen, Terry, Christopher and Caroline Lindvall (for our family pilgrimage to Yellowstone); Brooke and Craig Ebel, and Dan and Cindy Schott Hunter (for joyful wedding celebrations—and our long talks); Dave, Shari, CeCe and Caroline Meserve (we couldn't have done it without you guys); Danielle Miller (thrift stores—and so much more); Jon, Stephanie and Brennan Link (faithful, faithful friends, through every season of the soul); Mary Shoaff (for thirty years of remembering your story, my story—and the moment we met the Story). This workshop of soul poets dances to the heartbeat, for sure.

Lastly, I'm grateful beyond words to my husband, Scotty Sawyer, for writing God's poetry in so many lives—including my own—so strongly, consistently and lovingly. This dance is for you.

Featured Poets

All client examples are used with permission of the client. Names and identifying details have been changed.

Grateful acknowledgment is made to *Inklings* and the *Mars Hill Review*, where earlier versions of portions of this manuscript first appeared.

Margaret Avison: "Person, *or* a Hymn on and to the Holy Ghost" from *Selected Poems* by Margaret Avison. Copyright © Margaret Avison 1991. Reprinted by permission of Oxford University Press Canada.

"March Morning" from *sunblue,* published by Lancelot Press, 1978, now distributed by Brick Books via General Distribution Services, 1-800-805-1083. Reprinted by permission.

Scott Cairns: "The More Earnest Prayer of Christ" used by permission of George Braziller, Inc.

Judith Deem Dupree: Section from "Rhythms" and "Road out of Kosovo" printed with permission of the poet. "Shadows of God" first appeared in *ProCreation* and was awarded first prize in its annual poetry contest. Reprinted by permission of the poet.

Derrel Emmerson: "Potato Christ," "Rhythms" and "Beethoven, Unborn" printed by permission of the poet. "Divorced" first appeared in the *Mars Hill Review* and is reprinted with permission of the poet.

Robert A. Fink: "On Jesus, Taking His Word on Immortality," first appeared in *Michigan Quarterly Review* 22 (1983) and is included in *The Ghostly Hitchhiker,* copyright © 1989 by Robert A. Fink, Corona Poetry Series, P.O. Drawer 12407, San Antonio, TX 78212, and *Odd Angles of Heaven: Contemporary Poetry by People of Faith* (Harold Shaw Publishers). Reprinted by permission of the poet.

Judith Gillis: "Lost and Found" printed by permission of the poet.

Ruth Goring: "Revision" first appeared in the *Mars Hill Review* and is reprinted by permission of the poet.

Carlene Hacker: "The Silent Burn" printed by permission of the poet.

Billie Ruth Hopkins-Furuichi: Haiku printed by permission of the poet.

Andrew Hudgins: "Christ as a Gardener" from *The Never-Ending.* Copyright © 1991 by Andrew Hudgins. Reprinted by permission of Houghton Mifflin Company. All rights reserved.

Kristy Johnson: "Luke 8:8" first appeared in the *Mars Hill Review* and was awarded second place in the annual *Christianity and Literature* student writing contest. "The Dilemma of Taking Up a Cross" first appeared in *ProCreation* and is reprinted by permission of the poet. "To Prove the Catch" printed by permission of the poet.

Denise Levertov: "What the Figtree Said" from *Evening Train.* Copyright © 1992 by Denise Levertov. Reprinted by permission of Laurence Pollinger Limited and New

Now is the shining fabric of our day

Torn open, flung apart, rent wide by love.

Never again the tight, enclosing sky,

The blue bowl or the star-illumined tent.

We are laid open to infinity

For Easter love has burst His tomb and ours.

Now nothing shelters us from God's desire—

Not flesh, not sky, not stars, not even sin.

Now glory waits so He can enter in.

Now does the dance begin.

"Opening" by ELIZABETH ROONEY

One

························ ❧ ························

Living by Poetry

The Creative Process of
Spiritual Growth

Every man will be a poet if he can.

HENRY DAVID THOREAU

W e live in a culture hard-driven by the need for answers.

Daily we encounter bright-yellow road signs that promise to point us toward spiritual and emotional success, clearly mapped routes that can be easily marked and measured and, ultimately, graded. We're guaranteed tangible results right now, on freshly laid blacktop, with crisp, white center lines.

We're offered Ferrari-fast solutions. And sometimes they work.

But why do "ten easy steps to (fill in the blank)" rarely orchestrate the richer, fuller soul-symphonies we long to live? And why does the surround sound of "how to" rarely attune us to a frequency higher than ourselves?

Maybe it's time to put the brakes on our drive toward answers. Time to turn off the dull, throbbing, high-powered stereo of pragmatism. Time to hop out of this car headed fast toward spiritual nowhere—and start break dancing to some different music. Kick off those ill-fitting corrective shoes . . . and begin dancing to the heartbeat of redemption.

After all, we read in Scripture that "we are God's workmanship"— God's creative artwork, his poetry (a concept we'll examine later). Throughout his Word he hints that we're fashioned for more than just fixing our marriages or troubleshooting our businesses. More than even achieving a successful spiritual life. God the Poet invites us to his passionate opera of faith, hope and love; his exquisite, delicate ballet of both pleasure and suffering; his moody, prophetic jazz wafting through the world.

Living as God's poetry is countercultural in a society that largely neglects the mission of loveliness, of being. "The heavens declare the glory of God," the psalmist exults (Ps 19:1 NIV). The stars in the sky are glory, he tells us. Simple enough. They perform no duties except the work of being beautiful for the enjoyment and glory of the Creator.

That poetic beauty is, in itself, a calling. As the poet e. e. cummings says, "Poetry is being, not doing. If you wish to follow, even at a distance, the poet's calling . . . you've got to come out of the measurable doing universe into the immeasurable house of being."[1] This "house of being" cummings sets before us is a broad, inviting space of visionary living. Poetry isn't a way of saying things—it's a way of seeing things.[2]

That's why entering the creative house of being cummings describes won't cause us to stop all our activities and do nothing. (Imagine what would have happened if Jesus had decided just to sit tight in his snug world and "be.") Rather, the energy of being God's poetry empowers us to do *more* than we ever dreamed possible. It means, simply, that we *see everything—including what we do*—differently, because we're becoming different people.

This sort of being—and becoming—is living by poetry.

Living by Poetry

Judith, an attractive, brown-haired twenty-five-year-old, called me to see if we could talk about our mutual interests of poetry and faith. When we met, I noticed immediately that my new friend was—as she still is—a woman of enormous passion and conviction. She had immersed herself in missions work in Guatemala and El Salvador. She had also been actively involved with impoverished communities in inner-city Washington, D.C.

Yet, strangely, Judith's eyes were flat, lifeless—a woman struggling on the razor's edge of depression. I grew curious about this paradox of a woman sitting cross-legged in front of me.

As she tucked her feet underneath her on the couch, Judith told me more about her creative interests. Together, she and a friend had recently read several books that challenged them to connect their spiritual lives with their artistic interests. Before she'd departed on a visit to Guatemala, Judith and her friend had committed to writing each other once a week for the full twelve weeks of the trip. The result was more than she could have hoped for: their mutual forays into fun word play had whetted her creative appetite. Soon after she returned home, Judith's writing slowly began to take a poetic form.

Yet there were obstacles to this new writing passion. One had to do with the conviction Judith felt to work with the poor. In her latest ministry venture she'd come face to face with a hard truth: she wasn't able to claim her experiences with the poor as her own. She felt that she needed an even deeper sense of conviction—that there were even more alive parts of her soul that remained unexplored, untapped. For this reason, she felt, not only did she not have an authentic voice with the poor, but she was also afraid that she didn't have a voice of her own—one that was connected both to God and to the world, one that contributed to the larger good. Now, Judith wondered, was her new desire to "have a voice" prideful? After all, who was she to pursue a different spiritual life than the one she'd always known?

Another of Judith's obstacles was a typical one for budding writers. When she first started keeping a journal, all her entries began with "Dear Lord" or "Dear God"—a safe sort of piety. But as she continued, she committed herself to gut-honest writing—the kind that didn't see God as an editor peering over her shoulder—and her imagination had begun to flow. Soon she awakened to a new and much more complex Judith. But now she had to wrestle with some very unsettling questions: Was God pleased by her new honesty, or was he upset by it? If he was upset, could she bring herself to abandon the writing? (She knew she couldn't.) Or could she abandon God? (Never.) She wasn't finding answers, only more difficult questions.

On that day we met, we talked about journeying together into the unknown territory in Judith's spiritual life. One possibility, we concluded, was that poetry might serve as a vehicle for the journey. Neither of us knew where poetry might take her, but it seemed clear this was a creative pilgrimage she was meant to make.

Judith took the first step on that journey by showing me some of the poems she'd written before we met. Here is one of those earlier works:

Dancing with God
Imagine a man and woman
famous for their passionate tango—
experts in rhythm,
partners in grace—

locked immobile
in a fierce embrace
as each one whispers
"let me lead!"

It was a simple poem, but it stated in a fresh way our common, life-long, ballroom struggle to let God lead.

Judith's questions continued. Even as her verse flourished, she wondered, Is poetry useful? Isn't it wasteful to spend time writing poems in a world filled with starving, hopeless people? I encouraged her to keep exploring, keep asking questions, and continue trying to find a voice for her struggles. During this time she showed the following poem to me, a story about one of her missions ventures:

Refugees
We wait
dusty and hot in Comalapa
til the battered Ford truck lumbers up.

"Get a seat,"
someone says to the gringa, so I
slurp up my Orange Crush and clamber on.

Fifteen or more
Guatemalans pack in, shoving
bags of beans, rice, cabbage, soap on the flatbed.

Swaying, half-perched
on a board, I wrap my arm
round a little girl whose name, she says, is Máricielo.

Soon she slides
down to sleep on the floor,
her body filling the small space like water.

The older bodies stand stiff
against the roughness of the ride. We are silent,
for what words can speed the journey,
or make home

the destination? A road has been cut
through the jungle, but not by these travelers.

And Maricielo sleeps
easily there on the rattling floor.
Like Jesus in his tossing boat.

Judith's poem offers a startling image of faith: the ease of a child's sleep in the midst of harsh circumstances. She compares it to Christ's ease when he spoke to the storm, "Peace, be still." By this time Judith's use of imagery and rhythm was growing clearer, more precise, as evidenced in lines such as "bags of beans, rice, cabbage, soap on the flatbed." We lurch alongside her in the truck and stiffen ourselves for the ride.

As she continued to create, Judith realized that the poems themselves weren't answering her deep questions. But they *were* plunging her beneath the surface of the people around her, helping her to return to a sense of wonder at common, everyday events.

For example, Judith used poetry to begin remembering and redeeming the stories of her family. In the following poem she beautifully portrays her father's music as his means to escape poverty, heat, ignorance and his brothers' tragic deaths:

Texas Prelude
I watch my father, age sixteen,
lie down each night on some new bed
in Kilgore, Lubbock, Goliad

and steer his neon radio
through static waves in search of friends:
Vivaldi, Mozart, Brahms. And then

begin to swing his arms, conduct
with glowing cigarette baton
some allemande or fugue, as if

such music can beat back the sun,
drown out the scream of junebugs, halt
the death of one more brother   or

push up beneath those flapping arms
in measured gust until you rise,
you fly, you leave it all behind.

This reflection of her musician father's youth reveals Judith's sense of wonder in the ordinary, as well as the unconditionally loving eye of the poet. She imaginatively enters into her father's story and captures an intimate moment in time. She also experiments with new poetic forms: she imitates the precise, ordered beats of her father's musical conducting through a poem written entirely in iambic tetrameter.

As she did with this poem, Judith happily experimented with various forms and styles of writing. She played with language, shuffling words and ideas like playing cards in a variety of combinations. At the same time her soul stretched and played as well. She pursued her relationships—and her faith—with more passion.

As Judith's love for poetry grew, she took a risky step: she applied to an M.F.A. program to study poetry full-time, and she was accepted. Her decision was a bold one. She uprooted her life to pursue a vision both creative and spiritual, one that gave her no solid guarantee of life direction or income. While immersing herself in this new, other world of poetry, she wrote of a revelation: "Through reading poetry in church coffeehouses, I've discovered I have a much more effective and provocative opportunity to share my concerns about political and social justice issues. . . . Poetry seems to reach people, while dialogues where 'buzzwords' like injustice, conservative, etc. are used just seem to close people's minds."

Judith had discovered a common ground for her passions of poetry and social justice. Yet poetry was—and is—too beautiful and mysterious to allow her to land in one place for too long. The following poem is a glimpse into a foreign tragedy that transported her to even deeper questions:

The Boat
Local ferry
drowned off the coast:
at least 300 people are dead.
Commuters to the capital from the island,
none of the passengers knew how to swim.

Write the poem
like you're building a boat:
hollowed out, planked together, pitched with tar.

100 yards from shore,
passengers rushed the ship's bow,
overwhelming the men paid to carry them
on their shoulders to shore.

Balance the hull and raise the mast,
let the mainsail curve to the wind.
Go beautiful and swift my boat.

A woman set off the stampede
when her infant son started choking.
The mother tried to push to the front
but the others refused
to let her through.

Steer straight into the gale—
don't let the rigging slack—
lean hard against the boom—

Three times the Ministry of Transport
has built a dock for the ferry—

each time hacked up and burned
by the carriers, whose income depends
on the off-shore landings.
The U.S. Ambassador cites the tragedy
as another example of the country's
inability to govern itself.

My boat my perfect boat you are too late.
You are not strong enough
to carry the dead.

And I cannot swim in these waters.

The poem concludes with Judith's sense that her poetry drowns in the face of such tangled suffering. The sinking of the boat, the choking infant and desperate mother, the rich country's judgment of the poor country's inability to govern itself—all lead her to a difficult place: how inadequate poetry—her "boat"—seems in the wake of human misery. Judith finds herself at sea, adrift as to how her writing can respond to such sorrow and injustice in the world.

Judith hasn't found clear answers for her questions through poetry. She has simply let the questions take her by the hand and lead her into a richer, more creative—and perhaps more devout—spiritual life. Writing poetry has helped her venture into more expansive countries in her heart, beyond the restrictive borders of barbed-wire, how-to answers. She's allowed poetry to teach her what it means to love both God and people from even deeper parts of her soul.

Not everyone is called to pursue poetry as literally and thoroughly as Judith Terry McCune has. But everyone is invited to participate in God's poetry workshop. Everyone is invited to become a "poet of the soul"—to see our lives through the prism of God's surprising, artistic design for his people. I call this *living by poetry*—the creative process of spiritual growth.

The Celts called this kind of spiritual journey *peregrinatio*. The word's meaning is illustrated in a story of three ninth-century Irishmen whose boat drifted at sea until it landed on an English shore. When the men were brought before King Alfred's court and questioned about their intended destination, they explained that they "stole away because we wanted for the love of God to be on pilgrimage, we cared not where."[3]

Peregrinatio is an inner pilgrimage that's embarked upon from a deep conviction yet is not headed toward a tangible place of spiritual "arrival." It is a poetic journey undertaken simply out of love for Christ.[4] Creative spiritual growth is the process of becoming more like Jesus.

We Are His Poem

In that gracious, large-hearted book of the Bible called Ephesians, the apostle Paul describes God and his people artfully. Paul marvels that we, the people of God, are creative works of art, and that God is the Artist: "For we are God's workmanship *[poiēma]*, created in Christ Jesus to do good works, which God prepared in advance for us to do" (Eph 2:10 NIV).[5]

This idea of human beings as works of art leaps to life when we look more closely at the Greek word Paul uses for "workmanship." *Poiēma* literally means "poem." Here, in living language, Paul describes us as God's own poetry—his image-laden, rhythmic, voice-saturated expression of himself.

The concept of God as artist complements another passage from Scripture. In Isaiah 45 God tells us he is a Potter and we are the clay, earthen vessels of his molding (v. 9). In God's vast pottery shop our lives and faith spin on the wheel of his artistic creation.

As one theologian remarks of the Ephesians passage, "The picture invites us to think of God in some great [artistic] workshop, and asks us to watch him forming and fashioning and bringing something into being."[6] In this scenario God is the consummate Craftsman, shaping us, his people, into various art forms for his purposes.

God's creatively constructed household of faith resembles an art gallery. In it we see odd, brightly painted Picassos displayed next to richly textured Monets. We're all his inspired masterpieces of love, carefully honed works in progress, created for his great pleasure and glory.

Here it all is, in living Scripture: God's artistic expression to the world isn't limited to his natural creation—mountains, sunsets, oceans. He has written his people, forming us line upon line so that we express his nature. "You are a letter of Christ," the apostle Paul says, ". . . written not with ink, but with the Spirit of the living God, not on tablets of stone, but on tablets of human hearts" (2 Cor 3:3 NASB).

Living as God's poetry isn't necessarily a mystical experience. It's something we're all capable of. Poetry, says Charles Angoff, "is the response of our innermost being to the ecstasy, the agony, the all-embracing mystery of life. It is a song, or a sigh, or a cry, often all of them together. Thus, we are really all poets."[7]

Those who live by poetry seek love and wonder amid a world daily in pursuit of cold, concrete answers and directives. They savor the simple, whole-grain flavor of hope, the stunning wine of grace. They dare to dip their toe, then possibly their whole foot, into the wide wading pool of their limited understanding of faith, eventually allowing themselves to be submerged in ripples of mystery.

Living by poetry means a willingness to be bamboozled by God.

Dislocating Our Faith

T. S. Eliot writes that the purpose of poetry is to "dislocate language into meaning."[8] Poetry shakes up our senses so that we read familiar words in new, enlightening ways. In the same way, living poetically can help dislocate our faith into meaning when we desperately need a renewed sense of it.

The poems you'll read in this book are primarily poems of belief, but that's not because I think poetry needs to be overtly Christian in order to have worth. Rather, it's because "poetry can rescue language from indifference."[9] And what language forever needs rescuing more than the language of our faith?

The poet Samuel Taylor Coleridge says that "the greatest truths we know 'are too often considered as *so* true that they lose all the life and efficiency of truth'; the task of the poet is to state the truth in a fresh way."[10] Jesus did this with his poem-parables: he dislocated the well-worn religious truths of his time into engaging stories, full of flesh-and-blood meaning. Even the greatest truth we know can often lose its vibrancy within us. It's then we most need a fresh view through the eyes of a poet—or the Poet.

I once heard someone say that people write poetry to find God. Perhaps that's true. But my hope in writing this book is that poetry could, in its own imaginative and immutable way, find *us*—and write God anew across our beauty-starved souls. May Christ grant us, as the title of this villanelle by Kristy Johnson implies, fertile heart ground that yields a hundredfold. May Christ the Poet gift us with "ears to see the poetry."

Luke 8:8

". . . because in times like these to have you listen, it's necessary to talk about trees." Adrienne Rich

Some have ears to see your speaking trees,
Chosen ones who feel a deeper power,
The few with ears to see the poetry.

The village god says, "Speak to those asleep,"
Broadcast a pleasant picture, paint flowers;
For they have ears to see you're speaking trees.

Listeners find truth in evergreens
And know why in winter lilies cower.
They are few with ears to see the poetry.

To some, storms are just weather surging seas;
To them seeds thrown may simply yield a bower.
They have ears to see you're speaking trees.

We are the few who become changing leaves,
Who through storms have longed to know The Bower.
The ones with ears to see The Poetry.

He gave the deaf and blind pure artistry.
The rest know better than to stay purblind.
Some have ears to see you're speaking trees,
But few have ears to see the poetry.

KRISTY JOHNSON

Two

....

Dancing to the Heartbeat
of Redemption

Poetry & Faith

---

*We must learn to feel with our minds
and think with our hearts.*

ELIAS CHACOUR

W hen my husband, Scotty, and I were first married, I used to tell
him I would jump up and down the moment I read a poem in the
New Yorker I actually *understood*. Once after watching me stare for a
prolonged period at a single page, he sat next to me on the sofa and
asked, "Are you still trying to read *that poem?*" I nodded. But by that
time we both realized it was a futile task.

Please tell me I'm not the only one.

Sometimes poetry seems incomprehensible, unobtainable, almost
like a foreign language. Its often obscure meanings and strange

speech can be intimidating. Yet the good news is that fully *under-standing* a poem isn't always the point of reading it. In fact, as one poet notes, "Poetry gives most pleasure when only generally and not perfectly understood."[1]

This bit of wisdom is good advice for those who want to explore how poetry relates to their spiritual life. When we read a poem, we might enjoy an image here, a certain rhythm there, or maybe even the title of the work. But the ultimate aim in reading poetry isn't simply to comprehend its meaning.

The poet Emily Dickinson writes, "If I read a book and it makes my whole body so cold no fire can ever warm me, I know that is poetry. If I feel physically as if the top of my head were taken off, I know that is poetry. These are the only ways I know it. Is there any other way?"[2] Dickinson is describing the *incarnational experience* of poetry. And her warm words are precisely where poetry intersects with faith: poetry is the shining grandeur of ideals fleshed out in the coarse wooden stable and swaddling clothes of words and images. We'll never fully understand why Christ came to earth in such an unorthodox manner. Yet we don't necessarily have to understand this unorthodoxy to love and follow Jesus.

The same is true of poetry. We can be content to relish the clash-and-bang sound of syllables, the ebb and water-flow of stanzas, the arresting pictures painted by crisp, clear images. Poetry isn't a lecture or a systematic explanation. It means to send us happily tap-dancing, or to lull us into comforting sleep, or to make us gasp in sharp recognition. We don't have to understand every word of it. But that's one reason poetry is so frightening and elusive: it is mysterious.

A bit of philosophy might help here. Gabriel Marcel draws a distinction between what constitutes a mystery and what constitutes a problem. A problem, he says, is an obstacle firmly rooted in what can be seen, felt, heard. A mystery, on the other hand, is something entirely different. It is something "in which I find myself caught up, and whose essence is therefore not to be before me in its entirety."[3]

We often feel uneasy when we don't understand something. In fact, we often view it as a problem rather than as Marcel's mystery. And that's one reason why some of us don't read poetry: we don't know what to do when we intuitively know something important is being said but we can't crack the code of its meaning. We're afraid to be "caught up," as Marcel says, and not understand why.

Yet isn't God like poetry in this way? He's mysterious. Like poems, we don't really "get him" sometimes, either. His ways are far beyond our limited understanding and logical comprehension. That's not to say a cognitive knowledge of God—or poetry—isn't important. After all, the best poetry, like the most compelling faith, is both fiercely thoughtful and thoroughly passionate. "In the beginning was the Word," writes the apostle John, "and the Word was with God, and the Word was God" (Jn 1:1). God is the Word, the Logos, the "living logic"—thoughtful logic imbued with passionate life. Of course, God speaks to our minds, but he also desires to affect our entire being—minds, hearts and souls.

In his book *The Idea of the Holy,* theologian Rudolf Otto talks of this experience as the *numinous* aspect of faith. By this he means that "the rational and moral is an essential part of the content of what we mean by holy or sacred: only that it is not the whole of it."[4]

Otto often describes this as "the numinous *feeling.*" However, his German translator, John Harvey, tells us Otto isn't using the word *feeling* as something "equivalent to emotion, but as a form of awareness that is neither that of ordinary perceiving nor of ordinary conceiving." Harvey notes that Otto's concept of the numinous is regarded as a way to describe the aspect of God that transcends or "eludes comprehension in rational or ethical terms."[5]

When our lives feel too pragmatic, too dry, too easily described, the *numinousness* of poetry can help us regain a sense of wonder. And that's where poetry and spiritual growth have something in common. Like writing a poem, spiritual growth begins with something that eludes mere rational comprehension. It begins by daring to follow what we cannot see with our eyes. It begins with faith.

Here the poet Robert Fink illustrates this mysterious connection:

On Jesus, Taking His Word on Immortality

Not a question of belief.
The Bible says even devils believe
and tremble, their humped backs smoldering
still, horns curled black
recalling the jagged heat of light,
the length of a scream falling.
It is, instead, a matter of faith:
saying to the mountains, Move!
telling a cripple rise up and walk,
or doing what we do as if
each story were being written down
somewhere in red letters. It is patience:
learning to watch for the sea
to sift mountains down to size
thin enough for pockets
or skimming flat across the water.
It is waiting for the man to give it up—
the old alms game, eyes hard behind dark glasses,
one leg folded back until the night
and home down alleys narrow as the eye of storms.
Can we count the hairs of a head?
Or clothe ourselves in lilies?
It is harder than belief.
It is what we pray to find at the end of poems.

ROBERT A. FINK

As the poet says, faith is what "we pray to find at the end of poems." It is the substance we hope for, the creative evidence of things not yet seen. And that is how the spiritual life of the soul poet begins: by trusting that there is a creative idea worth following, worth pursuing—and that there is something to discover at the end of life's poem.

Poetry Linked with Faith

God chose to tell his story and the story of his people's lives largely through poetry. Nearly two-thirds of the Bible is written in some poetic form of the Hebrew and Greek languages: the Psalms, Proverbs, Song of Solomon, Lamentations, the books of the Prophets, Revelation. Even the highly structured, stringent laws and regulations of Leviticus contain poetry.[6]

Jesus used colorful stories to convey much of his message. Surprisingly, of all literary genres, poetry most closely resembles Jesus' parables.[7] In fact, some of his language could be considered the street poetry of its day. Now there's something to ponder: Jesus as rap artist, one who spoke to the beggar-hearted through the rhythms and images of his own culture. Not only that, but even Christ's withholding poetry—as he deliberately did many times with the proud, self-righteous Pharisees—was also a means of communicating his message.

"Blessed are those who hunger and thirst for righteousness," he poeticizes on the Sermon on the Mount, "for they will be filled" (Mt 5:6). Lilting, lovely words of hope, spoken in rhythmic cadences. Jesus' green-grass-patch Rap on the Mount is reminiscent of a poem by Andrew Hudgins, in which he offers us a most earthy view of the Poet:

Christ as a Gardener
The boxwoods planted in the park spelled LIVE.
I never noticed it until they died.
Before, the entwined green had smudged the word
unreadable. And when they take their own advice
again—come spring, come Easter—no one will know
a word is buried in the leaves. I love the way
that Mary thought her resurrected Lord

a gardener. It wasn't just the broad-brimmed hat
and muddy robe that fooled her: he was that *changed.*
He looks across the unturned field, the riot
of unscythed grass, the smattering of wildflowers.
Before he can stop himself, he's on his knees.
He roots up stubborn weeds, pinches the suckers,
deciding order here—what lives, what dies,
and how. But it goes even deeper than that.
His hands burn and his bare feet smolder. He longs
to lie down inside the long, dew-moist furrows
and press his pierced side and his broken forehead
into the dirt. But he's already done it—
passed through one death and out the other side.
He laughs. He kicks his bright spade in the earth
and turns it over. Spring flashes by, then harvest.
Beneath his feet, seeds dance into the air.
They rise, and he, not noticing, ascends
on midair steppingstones of dandelion,
of milkweed, thistle, cattail, and goldenrod.

ANDREW HUDGINS

Hudgins's image of Christ as a hat-wearing, weed-pulling gardener is fresh and inviting. He holds the spade of seasons that unearths spring, then harvest. Beneath his feet as he ascends in the air, cattail and thistle seeds dance merrily to the heartbeat of redemption. His poem is a good example of how poetry—and Christ's poetry—can help us see our faith with new eyes.

Poetry connects with faith in yet other ways. The poet Karl Shapiro believes that "every good poet is a 'mystic'; that is, he departs from the dictionary, as the painter departs from the straight line and the perfect circle."[8] When an artist is familiar with the rules of his art— such as drawing lines and circles—they become second nature. He can then create his works of beauty more freely. He can be confident that, over time, no matter how outlandishly different his works may become, they'll always be undergirded by the artistic laws he learned early on.

Our faith is the same way. We study, digest and meditate on the laws of God until they become an integral part of the way we think and live. As we do this, a poetic framework of Scripture develops within us—an undergirding second nature that enables us to paint the colorful, richly textured kingdom of God across the "bleared, smeared" canvas of this world. We can creatively write and paint Christ's expression, in both broad brush strokes and painstaking penmanship. And sometimes in simple crayon scribbles and finger-paints. The operative word here is *creative*.

Over the years scholars and artists have also connected poetry with faith. They've detected an effortless ebb and flow between the two subjects: "Because of the 'imaginative wholeness' which is the source of the poet's vision, there is a distinct affinity between poetry and religion, for both religion and poetic expression are concerned with a heightened awareness and a sense of unity, and an attempt to find perfect expression for these qualities."[9]

This "heightened awareness and sense of unity" is one way we might describe our lives. We want to be fully aware of God. And we want to be unified with his purposes in the world. In short, we want God to find his perfect artistic expression in us and through us.

"The poet really does see the world differently," says Karl Shapiro. "He does not go into training to sharpen his senses; he is a poet because his senses are naturally open and vitally sensitive."[10] Likewise poets of the soul see the world differently because God's grace has cradled their souls, making their hearts open and sensitive to his love.

So in order to know more about God's poetry, we can pursue a simple question: What, exactly, do poets *do*—and how do they create?

The Poet's Process

The actual nuts-and-bolts process of composing poetry varies with each writer. Yet most poets agree that the germ of a poem usually begins *intuitively*. In the poet's eye a tiny or huge or merely medium-size detail in the world suddenly possesses a certain glorious magic or deep sorrow or bland apathy.

The Jesuit priest-poet Gerard Manley Hopkins savors the strange, lovely grace of the world's offerings in his poem "Pied Beauty":

Glory be to God for dappled things—
 For skies of couple-colour as a brinded cow;
  For rose-moles in all stipple upon trout that swim;
Fresh-firecoal chestnut-falls; finches' wings;
 Landscape plotted and pieced—fold, fallow, and plough;
  And áll trádes, their gear and tackle and trim.
All things counter, original, spare, strange;
 Whatever is fickle, freckled (who knows how?)
  With swift, slow; sweet, sour; adazzle, dim;
He fathers-forth whose beauty is past change:
                Praise him.

Hopkins captures the sheer pleasure of wildly different things on earth, taking worshipful delight in everything God has created, however odd they might seem: "We feel the poem opening out toward the celebration of the rich and quirky particularity of all things whatever."[11]

The poet ends, though, on a grand paradox: he says that the Source of this immense dapplery (color variations) is past change. In other words, even though the Creator has created millions of variations, he himself never varies. The poet then leaves us with a simple, open-mouthed summation to such awe-inspiring creativity: "Praise him." What more is there to say?

Hopkins's bright, confetti-worded poem illustrates what poets do. Poets burrow deep within their own fickle, freckled souls to carefully choose those sweet, sour, adazzle, dim images that best capture joy, pain, peace, loneliness, love, fear. They observe, they listen, they weigh, they judge, they appreciate, they relish, they draw truth from the fresh-firecoal of nature and their own couple-color lives to express universal truths about the human experience.

One of the poems I wrote in college was about my first experience reading Hopkins's poetry. I attempted what I've described above: to observe, to appreciate, to relish something beautiful in the world—this time, a poet I liked. I tried to capture the paradox of Hopkins's ascetic Jesuit life combined with his exuberant, crammed-with-passion poetry:

gerard manley hopkins:
your words-and-hyphens
smudged together
like child-dabbled
fingerpaints,

your simple
cassock
concealing
an erupting heart
of Glory,

your molten
self
contained,

restrained

by
a careful,
brown
life.

The artist in the corral

JOY SAWYER

The poem began with an intuitive response to Hopkins, a tiny seed of truth that his work and life planted deep within my heart. And when it comes to creating poetry, intuition is our beginning point. This is one of the stumbling blocks to poetry—including God's poetry—for purely pragmatic thinkers: a poem begins with an *internal* reality, not an outward one. In fact, one poet says that it's the rational person who is least able to understand poetry.[12] As with the writing of a poem, the faith life of the soul poet begins with a small germ, a tiny seed.

The Poetry of Obedience

The kingdom of God, Jesus says, is like a mustard seed planted in a garden. It eventually grows into a huge tree where birds make their home (Lk 13:18-19). From such a tiny mustard seed, the real, rich life of faith begins. The fruitful tree of our poetic obedience eventually sprouts from hidden, underground places.

The Greek word *poiētēs* (meaning, literally, "poet") is used several times in various New Testament epistles. Intriguingly, this word usually appears in the context of obedience. In one instance Paul tells us that "not the hearers of the Law are just before God, but the doers [literally, 'those who are poets'] of the Law will be justified" (Rom 2:13 NASB). A poet of the law, apparently, is someone who not only hears and knows the Scriptures but who also uses what he or she knows to develop into a rich artistic expression (or expresser) of God's commands.

Even works-oriented James uses the same word in reference to obedience. He writes that anyone "who listens to the word but does not do *[poiētēs]* what it says is like a man who looks at his face in a mirror and, after looking at himself, goes away and immediately forgets what he looks like" (Jas 1:23-24 NIV). The message here is mirror-clear: the reflection of our faith in the world looks, feels and tastes more like passionate poetry than it does rote, rhetorical actions.

The English word *obedience* stems from the Latin "to listen."[13] And living by poetry means that our love or righteousness or holiness results from the spiritual listening that occurs in the deep, unseen music room of the soul. Only then can the poetry of doing follow. Ultimately, the soul poet cannot help but express outwardly what's erupting in the hidden corners of his or her soul. That's when obedience is fluid, musical. Poetic.

However, living by poetry isn't a matter of self-will. We don't have to try to be good, or determine we'll somehow do better at this Christian thing. (Our valiant self-efforts ring hollow anyway, with all the artistic appeal of a black-velvet Elvis painting. When this happens, we can admit to ourselves and to God that our hearts are in a state of serious soul kitsch.)

Instead, those who live by poetry choose to look into the Word-mirror and remember its humbling reflection. And it's there we're liberated from self-effort: the Artist of our souls can transform black velvet into Breughel. Beauty is his business. As we see ourselves in the clear, truth-telling light of our blemished humanity, we're reminded that we're his work of art in progress. And we can yield our hearts to his loving craftsmanship in order for the creative process of spiritual growth to continue.

Often when we think of words such as *righteousness* or *obedience*, we think of dutiful, early-morning Scripture reading; self-sacrificing inner-city ministry; deferential loving of our neighbor as ourselves. And these things may indeed be righteous, obedient activities. But it's the *heart* behind our activity that's the focus of obedience in both the Ephesians 2 and the James 1 passages.

Living by poetry means dancing passionately to the heartbeat of redemption rather than shuffling to the humdrumming of a cold, austere performance of the law. The heart of the soul poet gives freely, loves extravagantly, lives poetically: "[God] throws caution to the winds," the apostle Paul says, "giving to the needy in reckless abandon. His right-living, right-giving ways never run out, never wear out" (2 Cor 9:10 *The Message*). In our own lives, such abandon to loving freely and generously comes from living by poetry—living by the lively *spirit* of the law.

In fact, when we live as God's poetry in the world, we appear as strange and unique and alive as the wart hogs at the zoo. We see this truth reflected in the way this writer describes poems:

Living Things

Our poems
Are like the wart-hogs
In the zoo
It's hard to say
Why there should be such creatures

But once our life gets into them
As sometimes happens
Our poems
Turn into living things
And there's no arguing
With living things
They are
The way they are

Our poems
May be rough
Or delicate
Little
Or great

But always
They have inside them
A confluence of cries
And secret languages

And always
They are improvident

And free
They keep
A kind of Sabbath

They play
On sooty fire escapes
And window ledges

They wander in and out
Of jails and gardens
They sparkle
In the deep mines
They sing
In breaking waves
And rock like wooden cradles.

ANNE PORTER

As God's living poems, we are rough or delicate, little or great. We wander in and out of both the restrictive jails and the fruitful gardens of our lives. We sparkle in the deep, hidden mines of our private sufferings. We keep a sacred sabbath and sing in breaking waves of praise.

"Surely there is something of heaven in holy poetry," writes the Puritan pastor Richard Baxter. "It charmeth souls into loving harmony and concord."[14] And surely there is something of heaven in those who embrace the holy calling of *poiēma*—who dare to dance to the heartbeat of the plainspoken parable-poet from Nazareth.

In the Twentieth Century
Christ, you walked on the sea,
But cannot walk in a poem,
Not in our century.

There's something deeply wrong
Either with us or with you.
Our bright loud world is strong

And better in some ways
Than the old haunting kingdoms:
I don't reject our days.

But in you I taste bread,
Freshness, the honey of being,
And rising from the dead:

Like yolk in a warm shell—
Simplicities of power,
And water from a well.

We live like diagrams
Moving on a screen.
Somewhere a door slams

Shut, and emptiness spreads.
Our loves are processes
Upon foam-rubber beds.

Our speech is chemical waste;
The words have a plastic feel,
An antibiotic taste.

And yet we dream of song
Like parables of joy.
There's something deeply wrong.

Like shades we must drink blood
To find the living voice
That flesh once understood.

James McAuley

Three

Conformed to
the Image of Love

God in a Red Wheelbarrow

*For those whom he foreknew he also
predestined to be conformed
to the image of his Son.*

ROMANS 8:29

I once worked as a writer for a religious television network. My roommate at the time, whom I'll call Carla, was a spot producer and on-air interviewer for the network. One of her projects included doing man-on-the-street interviews. With her camera and sound crew taping, Carla asked current-events questions of Wal-Mart shoppers or McDonald's diners, acquiring a cross section of quotes that would demonstrate common Americans' current trends in thinking. The nature of the questions Carla asked were designed to provide segues for the television program's evangelistic thrust, such as, "What do you think is the biggest problem our nation faces today?" or "How can we work together to improve our public school systems?"

One day while Carla was conducting interviews, she walked up to a well-dressed man and, with the cameras rolling, began talking to him. As soon as the man responded, however, it became painfully clear that he had a severe speech impediment. His handicap was so severe, in fact, that the crew stopped taping; they knew their footage of him would be unusable. But Carla continued to engage the man, and she motioned for the crew to resume shooting. She asked the man her entire list of questions, thanked him and then moved on to interview others.

The next week while at work, Carla received a phone call from this man. He had had difficulty locating her because none of the network's telephone receptionists could understand him. Finally he'd gotten through, and in painstaking, halting speech, he told Carla, "Thank you for what you did for me last week. I knew you couldn't use anything I was saying, but you made me feel like a worthwhile human being. I won't forget your kindness."

The phone call was, Carla told me, a profoundly humbling and eye-opening moment for her. In the midst of her work for this network—work that regularly reached millions each day with Christ's message of hope—God had used her soul's inner beauty to touch one man's heart. This stark contrast wasn't lost on her. In this instance my friend didn't help proclaim the message; she *was* the message. This man saw her flesh-and-blood life as a loving Word picture.

This subtle distinction is the vast difference between the predictable rhetoric of our lives' "religious language" and the surprising loveliness of poetry. It is also an example of one of poetry's most powerful devices—imagery.

The Power of Image

According to poet William Packard, author of *The Art of Poetry Writing,* poets need three basic skills in the practice and mastery of their craft: image, rhythm and voice.[1] These three poetic elements combined melt refrigerated words into buttery, creative life. Their smooth blend helps us make (even bake) a "poem." They are also parallel concepts to another poetic process: image, rhythm and voice are all tools for God's use in the poetry workshop of the soul.

In this chapter and the two that immediately follow, we'll explore each of these three powerful poetic elements and their relation to us as God's living poetry. For now, though, we'll focus on the unique tool of image.

Packard defines *image* as "a simple picture in words, a mental representation."[2] Not surprisingly, the best poetry is often image-driven as opposed to rhetoric-driven. It paints mental pictures for the reader rather than just providing information.

A classic example of image-driven verse is one of the most anthologized poems of the twentieth century, William Carlos Williams's short work "The Red Wheelbarrow":

so much depends
upon

a red wheel
barrow

glazed with rain
water

beside the white
chickens

Williams's poem succinctly displays the wonder of carefully cultivated imagery. The simple, stark picture of a wet, red wheelbarrow sitting next to white chickens paints a vivid image in a minimum of words. Just as we read that "so much depends" upon this image, so too we see that the whole poem *itself* depends upon it.

This poem's power as a "picture" is said to owe much to Williams's relationships with art and artists. He especially loved photography.[3] So it's not surprising that his poems would be filled with vibrant, full-of-life images. In fact, "The Red Wheelbarrow" is an example of *ekphrasis*—words representing a picture.[4]

In some aesthetic studies, such as W. J. T. Mitchell's *Iconology*, literature and visual arts are portrayed as *paragonal,* one fighting for dominance over the other.[5] In this poem, however, we see a perfect blend between words and "pictures," between poetry and the object of the poem. One doesn't try to overshadow the other; both work together to paint a verbal picture.

In the poetry workshop of the soul, we are much like the red, rainwater-dripping image we see in Williams's poem. Our Creator-Poet fashions us into just this sort of vivid, startling "Christ-picture." This picture works hand in hand with our faith words to paint within us a verbal image, an *ekphrasis* that can't be experienced in any of his other creations.

For example, several years ago a writer friend read a newspaper article about a young, up-and-coming Hollywood filmmaker whose work in the past had especially offended conservatives. In the article the filmmaker commented that Christians were the most arrogant people he knew, and that they'd done nothing but hurt him.

The man's remark saddened my friend. She immediately went to her computer and wrote him a letter, apologizing for the pain and rejection he'd experienced from believers. "I'd like to be a Christian who really cares about you," she wrote. Then she sent the letter and soon forgot about it.

To her surprise, the filmmaker called her a few weeks later and thanked her for the letter. My friend and this man soon began a written correspondence about a wide variety of mutual interests—literature, gardening, travel. He asked her questions about her faith, and she responded with questions about his. To this day their letters continue to cross the country.

My writer friend's story is a beautiful example of how words of faith and the image of Christ in a soul poet work hand in hand, in harmony—neither dominating the other. Both her faith words and the image of love reflected through them painted for this man a verbal picture. In other words, God shows up in the red wheelbarrow of our lives.

When we live by poetry, our lives slowly grow in ways that extend beyond mere rhetoric and theology. Because the Poet longs to craft his very own *image* within us, our "right answers" no longer seem adequate. Instead, we find ourselves longing to give poetic expression to a full-bodied faith, one that sometimes seems stifled by two-day seminars or three-point sermons alone. Of course, these things can be a heart poet's tools, but they remain a distant second to the mysterious, living image of the Poet-in-residence.

The soul poet's joy ripens from an ever-growing realization that the true poetry of his or her life takes place, as the apostle John says, not in words alone but in deed and in truth (1 Jn 3:18). Or in pictures. Poets long to see leaden rhetoric replaced by transparent images. Likewise, soul poets invite the Poet to continue his intricate craftsmanship so that the creative image of Christ replaces dull, predictable religion.

The poet Robert Bly says one of the great delights of poetry is that it helps us to remember relationships that are important. One of our roles as careful readers of poetry, he says, is to notice especially the work's images and to ask, "Does this image help me remember a forgotten relationship?"[6] As soul poets, we can ask ourselves a similar question about our life's poetry: "Does the Image in my life cause others to remember the forgotten Lover of our souls?"

. . . Person, or *a Hymn on and to the Holy Ghost*

How should I find speech
to you, the self-effacing
whose other self was seen
alone by the only one,

to you whose self-knowing
is perfect, known to him,
seeing him only, loving
with him, yourself unseen?

Let the one you show me
ask you, for me,
you, all but lost in
the one in three,

to lead my self, effaced
in the known Light,
to be in him released
from facelessness,

so that where you
(unseen, unguessed, liable
to grievous hurt) would go
I may show him visible.

MARGARET AVISON

The Image of Love

The primary Word picture painted within us by our Poet is the image of love. We love, John tells us, to our amazement, because the Poet first loved us (1 Jn 4:10). The heartbroken laments of the prophets, the creative teachings of Christ, the straightforward letters of the apostle Paul—all of these reveal glimpses of God's love-drenched heart toward his people.

Dorothy Sayers writes that God's "work of creation is a work of love, and that love is the most ruthless of all the passions, sparing neither itself, nor its object, nor the obstacles that stand in its way."[7] As God's people, we bear the marks of a relentless, passionate Love that withheld nothing, not even the death of his beloved Son. Love is the image of Christ, God's word picture written across our hearts.

It's this Christ-image of love burning within us, fueling our life poetry, that prevents our proclamation of the gospel from rambling into the weak, cliché-driven "clanging cymbals" of language alone. Our expressions of Christ's love reveal one of the poetic devices God uses to remind the world of his passionate care. The poet Diane Wakoski says, "Poetry is a human art, and we're really talking about our lives, and poetry which is most read is that which is most intimate and touching."[8] As soul poets, we learn that the poetry in our lives most read is love.

But like poetry, that love is not static, not rote, not stereotyped. The image of Christ's love looks different through each one of us, depending upon our current stage in the creative process of spiritual growth. God is always doing something new, because he's constantly conforming us into the image of his Son, of his love. Depending on the stage of each person's journey, that love might hug a neighbor child or head up relief work to refugees in Kosovo; it might quietly make ham sandwiches for the homeless or lobby loudly in Washington on behalf of the handicapped; it might either bandage bleeding wounds or tenderly uncover them. That's because the image of Christ's love is not easily pigeonholed or labeled. The poetry of love is expressed uniquely through each one of us.

Creative Risk Taking

In order to grow, poets take creative risks. They become vulnerable, experiment with new forms, dig deep for original thoughts. As soul poets, we take risks too—spiritual risks. It's dangerous to lead lives of power, conviction, creativity. These risks often take us beyond the borders of our own personal comfort and convenience. And necessarily so: Christ's image within us *transcends* what is humanly possible. The spiritual life burgeoning within us is the result of his power, not our own.

If we choose to live according to the risk-free law rather than the risky Spirit, our lives will read like trite, bad poetry. Just as any poem can suffer from a lack of imagery, so our lives suffer if a passionate, risk-taking love isn't one of our expressions of the Poet.

Ironically, such difficult risks require something simple—that we dare to come to God as little children: "Perhaps poetry, at least in certain aspects, requires a youthful state of spirit . . . [because] youth presupposes a capacity to love and to call forth love from others."[9] Living out the Poet's image means bravely loving others in creative, unorthodox ways—and calling forth love from them as well. It means clambering aboard love's rickety roller coaster and riding it to the hilt—trusting, letting go, sticking our hands high in the air as we rise and descend the sometimes unpredictable tracks of our hopes and fears. The ride of the Spirit is scary, yes, but it's also an adventure.

When we lose that childlike wonder, the poetry of our lives can seem obscure, stiff, *boring.* I love the prayer a poet friend of mine offered for our respective writing projects. She said, "Father, let us whoop and holler and ride our spiritual three-wheelers through the world with joy." Truly there is a beaming-face glory side to the divine image of Christ at work (or at play?) within us.

Yet there are other sides to the image of Christ—certain poetic risks. Despite the typical portrayal of Christianity, the image of Christ's love crafted within us is not necessarily slicked up, bow-tied and spit-shined. What it is, at all times, is honest and clear-eyed. The image of Christ within us empowers us to face bravely the harsh reality of a broken-down junkyard world, filled with snarling, yellow mongrel dogs. The image of his love within us is not only happily divine—it is also unashamedly human.

World-Weary Love

A former counseling client of mine, a fifty-year-old single woman named Betty, once told me a difficult story. Twenty years earlier while attending graduate school on the east coast, Betty had met the man of her dreams and fallen in love. They shared virtually all the same interests: hiking, biking, traveling. Both had even recently converted to Roman Catholicism.

On the day Betty thought this man was going to ask her to marry him, she got a rude shock instead. He said he was separated from his wife, who was living in another state with their four children, waiting for him to come home to them. He didn't want to.

Betty was stunned. She had no idea that the love of her life was married, let alone a father. Suddenly, her deep faith in God was assaulted. She agonized over what her relationship with the man should be.

Finally, she told him that, in good conscience, she couldn't continue to date him unless he tried once more to reconcile with his wife. Soon after their conversation, his work at the school they were attending ended, and he returned home with her words in mind. As it turned out, he and his wife eventually were able to patch up their marriage. They even had another child.

Twenty years later Betty unexpectedly ran into this couple at a business conference. Both the man and his wife thanked her profusely for her courage and her love, which had saved their marriage.

Yet this was the same reason Betty had decided to start seeing me. "I am still in love with him," she wept. "I know I'd still do the same thing all over again, but I miss him—even after twenty years." Her love for God—and for him—had cost her dearly. Hers was not a naive faith. Rather, it was one that entered fully into—and bravely faced—the sometimes painful, lived-out realities we suffer in a world of shattered dreams and constant loss.

As Betty's story illustrates, poets—and poets of the soul—also choose to face the world as it really is. Her story reminds me of how literary critic Babette Deutsch compares William Carlos Williams's image-driven poetry to the work of St. Augustine. Like Augustine, she says, Williams "sees the world arranged by an eloquence, not of words, but of things, many of them ugly. He can therefore accept the turd that the sparrows are sharing and the half-rotten potato on the plate."[10]

Accepting the turds and the half-rotten potatoes is part of embracing the humanity of Christ. He came and lived among us fully—frying fish, telling tales, weeping over deaths, doubting God's nearness. For us, bearing this human image means we choose to risk living—and loving— in a decaying world. Not to mention battling our own dark temptations.

That's why reflecting the human image of Christ means the simplest grace of all: acknowledging the deep shadow remaining in our own souls, and grappling with it, as he did. Before he faced the sheer horror of the cross, Jesus' prayer was not a glib "I'm glad this is happening, because it will all work together for the good of humanity." It was a struggle, a cry altogether different.

The More Earnest Prayer of Christ

And being in an agony he prayed more earnestly . . .
Luke 22:44

His last prayer in the garden began, as most
of his prayers began—in earnest, certainly,
but not without distraction, an habitual . . . what?

Distance? Well, yes, a sort of distance, or a mute
remove from the genuine distress he witnessed
in the endlessly grasping hands of multitudes

and, often enough, in his own embarrassing
circle of intimates. Even now, he could see
these where they slept, sprawled upon their robes or wrapped

among the arching olive trees. Still, something new,
unlikely, uncanny was commencing as he spoke.
As the divine in him contracted to an ache,

a throbbing in the throat, his vision blurred, his voice
grew thick and unfamiliar; his prayer—just before
it fell to silence—became uniquely earnest.

And in that moment—perhaps because it was so
new—he saw something, had his first taste of what
he would become, the first pure taste of the body, and the blood.

SCOTT CAIRNS

Like Jesus in the garden, sometimes we find ourselves in a squeeze play between what we know to be true theologically and what we struggle with emotionally and spiritually. We often face enormous pressure from others to not voice our feelings of pain, doubt, confusion, ambivalence.

However, that's usually the best time of all to meditate upon the dirt-under-the-fingernails humanity of Christ. It's also a good time to read a poem by the seventeenth-century clergyman poet George Herbert.

In "The Collar" Herbert allows us a peek into his spiritual struggle over the constraints of his pastoral calling. In this poem he has reached a place where he cries, "No more!" No more dutiful clerical obedience, no more submissive scriptural service. Instead, Herbert tells us, he wants some relief from all the pressure of ministry. He wants to get rid of the struggle and to wander happily through the big, wild, licentious world. And in the end, only a simple, nondescript encounter with holy tenderness can interrupt his fierce passion:

I struck the board, and cried, No more.
   I will abroad.
What? shall I ever sigh and pine?
My lines and life are free; free as the rode,
   Loose as the wind, as large as store.
      Shall I be still in suit?
      Have I no harvest but a thorn
      To let me blood, and not restore
What I have lost with cordial fruit?
      Sure there was wine

Before my sighs did dry it: there was corn
   Before my tears did drown it.
  Is the year only lost to me?
   Have I no bays to crown it?
No flowers, no garlands gay? all blasted?
   All wasted?
  Not so, my heart: but there is fruit,
   And thou hast hands.
  Recover all thy sigh-blown age
On double pleasures: leave thy cold dispute
Of what is fit, and not. Forsake thy cage,
   Thy ropes of sands,
Which petty thoughts have made, and made to thee
  Good cable, to enforce and draw,
   And be thy law,
  While thou didst wink and wouldst not see.
   Away; take heed:
   I will abroad.
Call in thy death's head there: tie up thy fears.
   He that forbears
  To suit and serve his need,
   Deserves his load.
But as I rav'd and grew more fierce and wild
   At every word,
Me thoughts I heard one calling, Child:
  And I replied, My Lord.

T. S. Eliot thinks that the reason most religious writing fails is because the writers write how they would *like* to feel rather than how they truly feel. "Of such pious insincerity," Eliot marvels, "Herbert is never guilty."[11]

We understand Eliot's wonder: Herbert's struggle is achingly genuine—as real as someone could possibly be about the work of ministry. In this poem the poet struggles fiercely with God over what is believed to be either his response to Christ's yoke (Mt 11:29-30) or his call to the ministry ("collar" representing the poet's clerical collar). Certain words Herbert uses have double or even triple meanings, and they may provoke multiple images associated with Christ: blood, tears, crown, thorn. When placed together, these images reflect on Christ's passion in Luke 22, as well as on various other biblical texts.[12]

Yet Herbert uses these same images to subtly underscore a great irony—that God continually pours out love toward his child, even as that child rants against the heavenly Father. Throughout "The Collar," the biblical references foreshadow Herbert's inevitable conclusion: "Me thoughts I heard one calling, *Child:* / And I replied, *My Lord.*" His tirade turns into the quiet trust of a young child who has nowhere to turn but to Abba's waiting arms.

Through this poem Herbert allows his life to serve as a picture of Christ's powerful image—even as he offers his broken humanity, including his rebellion. As Herbert offers up his soul as a work of art, the reader glimpses both the gorgeous brush strokes of the divine and the rude scribbles of human flesh.

Herbert's life as image tells the truth, and it does not, as Emily Dickinson's poem says, "tell it slant." He loves God, yet he is tempted *not* to love—and, in turn, he is loved all the more. Through his poetry he rips his soul wide open in front of us, and what we see in the end is a beautiful picture of Christ's love. This is the same sort of written vulnerability we see so often in that Old Testament poet and psalm maker David whenever he invites us smack into the middle of his chaotic heart. We get the full picture.

Yet even as George Herbert reminds us that our faith is both human and divine, the human imagery we see within both ourselves and others can be hard to accept. We have trouble, as poets say, "trusting the image"—allowing the picture of Christ's love within us to reveal what he desires.

That's because truly trusting the image requires not only the intangible work of the Spirit but also the tangible acceptance of our flawed humanity. To live in the tension of being a divine vessel (temptation: pride) and an earthen vessel (temptation: shame) is the paradoxical dance of belief.

The Dilemma of Taking Up a Cross
A Prayer

Lord, You have taken stubborn root in my natural
world, placed me between the rock and a wide path,

threatened destruction. If I speak to you or cuff
the rock with an ancient flowering wand,

you promise water, but my silence and rigid
repose yields, drips and trickles, never coming

to river. In a dream I see a sacred laboratory,
at the table, a Chardinesque still-life: cooked

grain lies without yeast, a beaker sits with measured
blood turned to alcohol, grits of dark in a sphere

of lamp light near charred lamb. A zodiac
circle of salt with bass head, eye glaring, one

eucalyptus branch on a Bunsen burner,
not consumed, disregarding physics. I will

eat and drink, but it must be weighed, calibrated.
There is no point to being merry. When I walk,

your breath forms ice on my shoulders, because of
this hunger, because I refuse aloe, because

I want to starve and burn and thirst, at least once
without you. In a holding place, nails and cedar

wait to be assembled, brought to bear, embraced.
Tools for the follower. I know the cost, so

emblems grow cobwebs and dusty in a closet.
Perhaps you'll wait for the taking up. Perhaps not.

.Perhaps I will take root, drink and follow.

Kristy Johnson

Living as the image of Christ means depending on the very human needs and desires the Poet-Artist uses to express himself in our lives. Yet that may be hard for us. What if he wants to honor himself through our human struggle to follow him, as he did through the poetry of George Herbert? We may already have designed our own tidy rhyme schemes of how we'd like his image to be crafted in us. But eventually our soul's transformation is the mysterious work of the Poet's hands, not ours. Our job is to open our hearts wide to his poetic work, his poetic words.

In short, living as Christ's image strips us of spiritual independence: "Blessed are the poor in spirit," says Jesus, "for theirs is the kingdom of heaven" (Mt 5:3). Blessed is the soul that realizes its poverty of the divine image of love, and that embraces its utter humanity, relying upon God even to *know* God, not to mention to be made like him in every way.

Blessed are the human poems who are vulnerable to the desires and wishes of the Poet, for theirs are the simple yet profound red-wheelbarrow images of love. And as William Carlos Williams writes so succinctly, "so much depends upon" the image alone.

Potato Christ
God was in Christ
surprising the world
which never imagined

He would come in burlap—
a potato person,
bread in a brown wrapper:
ordinary, accessible, every eater's food.

DERREL EMMERSON

Four

························

When Our Soul Sings the Blues

The Jazz Rhythm of Hope

---

*[The quality of poets] is not revealed
in the noble sentiments which their poetry
expresses, but in sensibility, control of language,
rhythm and music. . . .
Of course, work is tremendously important,
but, in poetry, even the greatest labour can only
serve to reveal the intrinsic qualities of soul
of the poet as he really is.*

STEPHEN SPENDER

Donald was our town gardener. During the arid, hot summers, brown clay pots would suddenly sprout like magic outside Berg and Pflasterer's Drugstore, Horlacher's Jewelers, Paden's Shoes, containers filled with scarlet and pink geraniums, bright purple petunias, ice-white daisies with butter-yellow centers. Day after scorching day, as the temperature inched above a hundred degrees and wilted both our parched lawns and our best outdoor intentions, Donald's brilliant flowers bloomed wildly all over town. His clay pots and carefully tended roadside gardens were burning bushes, neon-colored signs flashing cheerful messages to the world that, yes, something besides tumbleweeds *could* grow in western Kansas, if loved the way Donald loved his flower-children. There was hope for us all.

Donald was a short, shuffling man, about fifty or so. He owned only one outfit, it seemed—a dirty white T-shirt, with yellow stains under the armpits, and a pair of ill-fitting khaki pants. His face was brown, crinkled by the sun, and he wore science-professor glasses— dark on top, light on the bottom—which turned miraculously into sunglasses when the sun hit them just so. Winter or summer, he sported the same hairdo: a military-style crewcut.

For as long as any of us could remember, Donald had but one all-consuming job: to decorate Colby, Kansas, just as he would a beloved house. He lovingly spruced up sidewalks, painted the park with bright, symmetrically arranged plants, fussily arranged planters full of pansies and daffodils. The earth was his dwelling place.

Donald was a stutterer. "H-h-h-how's m-m-m-my g-g-girl?" he'd beam whenever I encountered him on our main street. "D-d-d-did you s-s-see my f-f-f-flowers?" The stutter quickly turned a brief conversation into a much longer one, as Donald shared his object of enthusiasm for the day. Perhaps he had acquired an Indian-head nickel for his coin collection at the local gun and coin show. Or a piece of Frederic Remington western art. Or maybe he'd received a letter from "J-J-J-eannie," his beloved niece in Alaska, whom he occasionally went to visit.

Donald was a permanent fixture in our family. All during my childhood my father claimed that my mother was an acquirer of strays: alley cats, homeless dogs, emotionally orphaned children, dazed alcoholics. Yet, although Donald, from all appearances, could have easily fit the category of stray, he was not. He was simply one of us. His place in our home was hard to describe—not really a brother or uncle or father figure, but more like a benevolent family elf. He was the silent, fumbling observer at birthday parties, the hunched-over figure in the bleachers at ball games, the huddled-up guest eating Mom's hamburger pie at dinner. He was part of every occasion no matter how large or small.

Since Donald lived in an apartment with a postage-stamp-sized yard, my parents decided one year to offer him a new paying job, one they thought he would enjoy: they bequeathed him our acre-sized, horrible-looking back yard, surrounded by wheat fields. In truth, my parents didn't expect much from Donald in the transaction. It was a gardening challenge of immense proportions.

For weeks and weeks that summer, though, Donald arrived every day before the sun came up and went to work feverishly on his knees amid the tenacious crabgrass and ragweed. We couldn't really see much of what he was doing, because a large clump of ragged bushes obscured most of the area in the yard he'd chosen to work on. Finally, way too early one morning, Donald burst excitedly into our living room, announcing to us all, "Y-y-y-ou c-c-can come l-l-l-look now."

When we stepped outside, we couldn't believe our eyes. Donald had transformed our sun-burnt jungle into a paradise of strange, sanctuary-like beauty: a granite rock garden with running water, pink roses and azure wildflowers. His vegetable patch sprouted every type of edible plant imaginable: huge pumpkins; shiny, purple eggplants; smooth-skinned cucumbers. He'd even converted the old, broken-down sandbox into a strawberry patch.

Donald had performed a transcontinental miracle: he'd turned a piece of Kansas prairie into a California oasis. He doggedly saw his invisible vision through to its colorful completion.

Today the memory of Donald's wildly blooming garden reminds me once again of some very simple poetic truths: the most beautiful flowers and most fruitful vines often erupt from the most unlikely patches of ground in our own lives. And the time that we are most desperate for a shining vision of loveliness is the moment when all we can see before us is a barren wasteland. Genuine poetic imagination—one that blooms with future promise yet remains firmly rooted in the realities of earth—is a rarity in our world.

Such imaginative living requires marching to the beat of a wholly different drummer, as Donald did. This is an entirely different rhythm of living. I call it "the rhythm of hope."

Rhythms

The poet listens for rhythms
and finds them where he can.
It takes a lot to hear rhythm where
rhythms are broken
or come staccato a' staccato
laid like meshes of nets
entangled in one another.
The modern world with its machines
breaks those rhythms or
imposes its own.

DERREL EMMERSON

From a literary perspective rhythm is a distinctive sense of sound, of timing. It finds its expression in the most common elements of life: the four seasons, the ebb and flow of the tide, the rising and setting of the sun. In fact, in the earliest written poetry the rhythm of a poem *itself* was believed to be indicative of a divine presence.[1]

Much good poetry is rhythmic, accentuated, metered. "The human soul, in intense emotion, strives to express itself in verse," T. S. Eliot says. "It is not for me, but for the neurologists, to discover why this is so, and why and how feeling and rhythm are related."[2]

In a poem rhythm is not what is said; it is *how*, even *when* it is said. Yet the metrical, seemingly ordered measurements of poetry's rhythm—iambics, anapests, dactyls, trochees and others—aren't necessarily laws per se. They're more like road markers that help us feel and describe the underlying pulse of the poem.

Even if we don't comprehend immediately the words of Edgar Allan

Poe's "Annabel Lee" or "The Raven," we feel these poems' dark moods simply by their droning rhythms. This is also why children adore Lewis Carroll's playful nonsense rhyme, "Jabberwocky" ("'Twas brillig and the slithy toves / did gyre and gymble in the wabe"). Even when the poem uses words that don't exist, we somehow still emerge from it laughing, *understanding,* even *seeing.* The poem's rhythms themselves communicate meaning—and perhaps even something beyond.

"From the poet's point of view," says poet Michael Ryan, "the rhythm helps the poem get written. . . . Rhythm and sound and arrangement— the formal properties of words—allow the poet to get beyond thought, or beneath it."[3] The rhythm is what undergirds the poem.

Beethoven, Unborn

I long to leave the liquid world
where vibration and gastric rumbles
whum around me. I am bound to feel,
to know the warmth of cramped spaces. Yet,
were I born deaf,
I would hear the song in myself and
see sights as colored sounds,
wild crescendos of color,
great vibrations of ocean force, which
translate to scores and clefts
to leave the deaf hearing
what I have felt.

DERREL EMMERSON

Longing for Rhythm

Poets aspire to create good rhythms: "The poet whose metrical effects actually work upon a reader reveals that he has attained an under-standing of what man in general is like," the literary critic Paul Fussell says. ". . . A great metrical achievement is more than the mark of a good technician: it is something like the signature of a great man."[4]

As one poet recalled of Duke Ellington's jazz lyrics, "It don't mean a thing if it ain't got that swing."[5] Poetic rhythm and meter aspire to musicality, to something that causes even plain words to dance, to sing, to *swing*. And in the same way, deep within our souls is a yearning to dance to the beat of imaginative, musical living. Denise Levertov speaks for us when she says, "The deepest listening, the ear of imagination, rejects all that merely *says*, that fails to *sing* in some way."[6]

Sometimes when a poem begins to form in my head, I receive the rhythm before anything else, even the words. I've heard other poets speak of similar experiences.

One friend of mine wrote this poem years ago while pounding the New York City pavement as a ghetto poet. The poem is based entirely on his congo drummer friend Ralphie's baroque drum improvisations of Afro-Cuban rhythms. Each syllable represents a beat of Ralphie's drum's "speech":

Drums from the Growing Ground
Tell it to me, Ralphie . . .
Ralphie, tell it to me under this lean tree . . .
Ralphie, tell me what's happening under the ground
That pulses the air lightly
Breaking these new buds
Over my head . . .

Tell me why drums beat
Out of the ground, Ralphie,
Tell me what a long winter it's been,
How the drum's talking itself alive,
How sweat (flows out of the ground, baby)
Makes leather sing . . .

What's that driving up through your feet, Ralphie . . . ?
Where were you all winter when I never felt you play . . . ?
Did you find some growing ground anywhere . . . ?

Tell me, Ralphie, please tell me summer's coming,
Tell me the ice is really falling off
These branches and your hands . . .

Tell me I'm gonna feel hot blood and sap
Pour down on me again this year,
And tell me there's gonna be wine enough for all our wounds . . .

Tell me I can splinter bottles with my tongue
Leaping from your drum,
And tell me how long till we die again, Ralphie,
'Cause every winter I'm on such cold ground, Ralphie,
such cooooold GROUND.

ANTON MARCO

As this poem shows, a rhythm may waft toward us before we ascertain what the poem itself means. We hear the rhythm of the poem—and grasp something of its intent—before we actually *understand* the poem.

Always on Time

Soul poets embrace the hope that God's rhythm—unlike our own—is always on time, always in perfect, measured beat to his purposes. The poet Antonio Machado says, "Poetry is the word *in time*" (emphasis mine). Our Poet is the Word in time—the one who faithfully brought us his word in time.

"Walk with me and work with me—watch how I do it," Jesus says. "Learn the unforced rhythms of grace" (Mt 11:17 *The Message*). Yet the unforced rhythms of grace—especially in a hopeless, cacophonous world—form a most peculiar, countercultural cadence.

This section from a longer poem by Judith Deem Dupree reveals the creative rhythm of spiritual growth:

Consider the way
when earthsmell and its crumble
comes to mind,
our fingers itch to furrow; or how
they drum
when our ears pound inwardly
to the flourish of a contrapunto.

But sometimes,
when our feet twitch, we cannot know
to jig into something larger.

Sometimes we choose
whatever rhythm comes to us.

Sometimes, "whatever rhythm comes to us" in life is the cadence of what we know is right biblically, but which logically we can't make sense of. If we're honest with ourselves, we'll admit we're often left in the dark about just where, in practical terms, this kingdom dance will ferry us. What should we do when we have no answers about which career path to choose? How should we approach a difficult family discussion? Give me the ten-point presentation, our souls beg. Show me the money!

Sometimes we do get immediate answers. Sometimes there are books, tapes, seminars—even Oprah—to "show us the money." Yet there are other times in our life when we can't see what's ahead of us. It's then that obedience to the rhythm can carry us. That's how we dance to the heartbeat of redemption. Like the rhythms of good poetry, our faith is read not merely as the cold facts, the practical *what* that is said: what job to take, how to solve a family problem. It is also read as the more mysterious *how* and *when* it is said. This is the Poet's way of telling us it's not answers we most need; the Spirit of the Poet himself will carry us through the questions.

When we have no practical answers, we still have the rhythm of God—the Spirit's work of hope—within our hearts. The Spirit's job is to remind us of the hopeful things Jesus has promised us. Sometimes those reminders come to us when we can't see one inch ahead of ourselves. He reminds us that what Christ calls blessed isn't what the world around us calls blessed. He reminds us that when our hearts feel most homeless, he's at work building our true home. He reminds us that his peace isn't anything like the world's sense of security.

The Spirit's jazz rhythm of hope—eternal hope—wafts through the grocery stores and kitchens and laundry rooms of our everyday existence. And because of that rhythm, we're invited to hear God in the bacon-and-eggs moments of life. Every conversation over lasagna is a possibility, a spiritual promise. Every ordinary moment of ordering take-out bean burritos; pushing a creaky, metal grocery cart; sorting dirty laundry; can become a door of vision and hopeful imagination.

off broadway
freddy brought the house down
praying in a laundromat
with a snaggle-toothed woman
in a large-print dress

freddy moved the audience
to their feet
as the suds & the tears
& the sweat
of the washer woman
mixed with the humid
air

freddy bowed low
for his performance
kneeling on the dirty floor

to the applause
of the rickety
dryers

& the Hosts
sang the chorus
again

begging freddy for more

& you know
he'll do it
again

time &
time
again

as the angels
forever urge him

encore
freddy

encore

JOY SAWYER

"Hope," says pastoral counselor Andrew Lester, "sees the present as pregnant, and it is curious about what might be birthed."[7] Hope is an expectant mother that one day will give birth to the life to come. And in order to fully connect to that future hope, we're invited to recall our faith stories of the past as well: "Hope is rooted in the past because we remember the mighty acts of God and our personal encounters with the transcendent. Hope is empowered from the future from where it receives its vision. Finally, hope is active in the present as it energizes and motivates us to live so that God's 'will be done on earth as it is in heaven.'"[8]

In order to truly have hope for the present and future, we're called to remember the goodness and mercy of God in the past—through his Word, our lives, the lives of others. The image of the four seasons can be helpful here: the rhythm of hope is the unexplainable belief that something organic, something seasonal is growing beneath the surface at all times, invisible to the naked eye.

Hope can accept the seasons of the soul because it embraces the growing process: "God's kingdom is like a seed thrown on a field by a man who then goes to bed and forgets about it," Jesus said. "The seed sprouts and grows—he has no idea how it happens. The earth does it all without his help: first a green stem of grass, then a bud, then the ripened grain. When the grain is fully formed, he reaps—harvest time!" (Mk 4:36 *The Message*).

The rhythm of hope means that any seed of the ripe Word has a life cycle all its own within us. God provides the environment of sun and rain; we remain in the soil of Christ's love, no matter what season of the soul we might be experiencing. God oversees the growth.

Directions for Spring
For Helen deVette

Watch the daffodils. Though they are not up yet,
already they are unstable, their high yellow
waving by the deep riverbed like a gang of suns.

Beware of how you plant them. Place the side marked
MADE IN HOLLAND down. Burn the box. Dig holes
at night and do not admit hope to your neighbors.

In winter, do not read Wordsworth, whose fields
permit riots of heat in the most implacable freeze,
whose breeze never stops shuffling pages of stamens.

Do not think of them in the dark, in basements,
while scanning the New York Times *on the rise of crime,*
or while making necessary arrangements with people.

Daffodils will take advantage. If one of them gets her green foot
into your last permanent room, nothing can follow but
bliss, crouching on every threshold, blocking all exits.

Should the strong arms of daffodils succeed in their terrible shove,
you will lose your last method of knowing sorrow:
you will recognize only love.

JEANNE MURRAY-WALKER

The Auditory Imagination

Poet Theodore Roethke recalls attending a reading by Robert Frost during which Frost stopped to quote an especially rhythmic line by Shakespeare. "Listen to that," Frost said in amazement, "just like a hiss, just like a hiss." In that moment Roethke remembered what Eliot calls "the auditory imagination." As Roethke explains it, this is "the sinuousness, a rhythm like the tail of a fish, a cadence like the sound of the sea or the arbor bees."[9] It is an imagination based on the *sound* of things.

Not surprisingly, "the auditory imagination" in the poetry workshop of the soul also comes to us through our ears: "So faith comes from *what is heard*, and what is heard comes through the word of Christ" (Rom 10:17, emphasis mine). Hearing the imaginative, living Word of God enables us to listen for the rhythm of his divine hope. It provides us with a musical score for our souls, one that resonates with beauty and hope even in the midst of chaos, when we may be singing the blues.

Roethke says of one of his own poems, "Rhythmically, it's the spring and rush of the child I'm after."[10] And that's the spiritual rhythm that we, as soul poets, aim for as well. Because of God's ultimately solid ground, we can ride his redemptive merry-go-round. We can ride out each season of the soul with expectant grace: "This resurrection life you received from God is not a timid, grave-tending life. It's adventurously expectant, greeting God with a childlike 'What's next, Papa?'" (Rom 8:15 *The Message*).

When our soul shivers in its frigid winter, bare branches clawing the sky, we remember that springtime brings fresh lilacs, warm breezes, times of refreshing. We recall that everything of beauty must first grow roots and push upward from the frozen ground. When we find ourselves in the midst of heart spring, we can enjoy and relish every moment, grateful that our desolate winters helped provide the fertile soil for our delight—and that we need not fear the ice when it arrives again.

Hope is the ever-deepening sense that, just as in nature, the human soul experiences its own changing seasons, tides, sunrises and sunsets—and that we are invited to fully participate in those changes, whether they're occurring in our own lives or in the lives of those we love. In fact, this is a sure sign that we're hearing the rhythm of hope—when we enter into the life seasons of others. We can wholeheartedly plunge into their blizzards of confusion and loss as well as celebrate their sunny cruises through fruitfulness and joy. We can rejoice with those who rejoice, and mourn with those who mourn (Rom 12:15).

The Silent Burn
For Lynn

Just yesterday our fingers ran the water's edge;
the breath of salt lay on our tongue.
We soaked in sun upon the shore
and felt liquid life flow over us.

Night comes too quickly.

The wind howls; the gulls beat their wings
like whips; the sea roils. Waves run wild.
They gather weight, lunge

upon the shore, and with a pull
as fierce and certain as a shark's jaw,
all we cherish is gone . . . taken . . .

simple things we held dear:
grains of sand, shells,
sight of bird's smooth sail,
a small castle made together.

If it were not for hope, the silent burn
too deep for the eye to see,
the mind to dismiss, the sea to consume,
we would be lost
to life's wash. But in the heat
of hope, the gull glides again
and soars, the sea rests, and sand
like old lace sifts through fingers.

Nothing dies.
Rekindled, it flames.

CARLENE HACKER

Living by poetry is the freedom to allow the seasons of our soul to come and go, trusting that the creative power behind them is at work, bringing all things to ripe fruition: "Being confident of this, that he who began a good work in you will carry it on to completion until the day of Christ Jesus" (Phil 1:6 NIV).

But such rhythm requires hope, real hope—not hope in the tumultuous realm of the circumstantial, but the continued trust that God's rhythm has its own carefully measured meter. Then hope is a relief, freeing us from the exhaustion of wheel-spinning striving. It means we can discard our hurried timetables, both for others and for ourselves. And instead we can be confident in the fact that God is at work in us, writing our life poems, and that we're simply coop-

erating in his fine-tuning of our phrases. I appreciate what the poet
Scott Cairns says in a recent interview: "God has already redeemed all
things; so why not feel pleased, assured, unhurried?"[11] Yes indeed.

Our part in the creative process of hope is simply to participate to
the fullest. Yet we participate with the restful understanding that a
magnificent tidal wave of redemption has already been set in motion:
"Poetry is rhythmic because the poet takes language at flood and
goes with it. He senses the wave of language."[12]

We may not be able to control the direction of the wave, but that
isn't our job anyway. Our main work is to ride that powerful, mysterious wave to the fullest, even if its culmination—the answers to our
hopes and prayers—occurs in the life to come.

Imaginative Neighbor Love

Genuine hope is not some sort of spiritual narcotic that aids us in
denying our earthly realities, especially our relational problems. As
Andrew Lester says, "Hope does not try to avoid the pain of finite
existence nor is it naive about suffering."[13] Hope is firmly rooted in
the earth. That's why ours necessarily has to get down-in-the-ground-
and-dirty when it comes to dealing with the pain we experience in
this life, especially in relationships. Blooming rose gardens are easy
for us to imagine. What's harder for us is to have a vision for one
another, especially when all we see are prickly thorns.

In her book *The Disciplined Heart: Love, Destiny and Imagination,*
philosopher Caroline Simon writes broadly on love in its varied
expressions, fleshing out her arresting concepts by exploring the
works of writers such as Flannery O'Connor, Leo Tolstoy, William
Kennedy, F. Scott Fitzgerald and Isak Dinesen. One of Simon's many
rich ideas is the concept of "neighbor love," the sort of hopeful vision
we're called to have for one another:

Neighbor love involves seeing a person as having a destiny even when
there is little overt evidence this is so. We can have neighbor love

toward people about whom we know little, or toward those we think are living in misguided or tragic ways. In neighbor love one is given, through grace, the creative imagination to see another as having a destiny even when all outward signs indicate otherwise.[14]

The very nature of love is to *expect* something from another.[15] To hope for creative change in someone—to imagine that beauty could emerge from a good line of poetry honed even better, a needless line removed—is the true, imaginative business of love. Such hope expects another's soul art to flourish, even if all we see is a poorly designed, paint-by-numbers person. Living out such tender, vulnerable hope, however, requires courage and perseverance. It requires belief in a portrait bigger than our own.

Listening to the rhythm of hope can help us avoid the "mistake of thinking that what we see and experience as reality is all the truth that exists."[16] Hope, like faith, is largely about what remains invisible in our lives: "Now faith is the assurance of things hoped for, the conviction of things not seen" (Heb 11:1). And that assurance of things hoped for is true in our relationships as well. As my friend Donald showed me, planting a colorful rose garden of true hope calls us to imagine creatively—without denying our tangled, ragweed realities.

"Be kind, tenderhearted, compassionate with one another," the Word drums to us, hoping our feet will skip to its beat, "forgiving one another as Christ has forgiven you" (Eph 4:32). The Scriptures sing to us a thousand other songs as well. And hope in God's powerful, moving, eternal orchestration helps us believe the message of that countercultural music now. In the midst of it all we might even savor a brief stanza rest of assurance that he'll someday reveal to us just how those small, quarter-note acts of obedience became a part of his symphony of praise.

"Let the peace of Christ," says Paul, "keep you in tune with each other, in step with each other" (Col 3:15 *The Message*). We stay in harmony with one another as we encourage each other about Christ's goodness, his faithfulness. When our soul sings the blues, hope is the smooth-jazz sound that still carries the tune.

What the Figtree Said

Literal minds! Embarrassed humans! His friends
were blushing for Him
in secret; wouldn't admit they were shocked.
They thought Him
petulant to curse me!—yet how could the Lord
be unfair?—so they looked away,
then and now.
But I, I knew that
helplessly barren though I was,
my day had come. I served
Christ the Poet,
who spoke in images: I was at hand,
a metaphor for their failure to bring forth
what is within them (as figs
were not within me). They who had walked
in His sunlight presence,
they could have ripened,
could have perceived His thirst and hunger,
His innocent appetite;
they could have offered
human fruits—compassion, comprehension—
without being asked,
without being told of need.
My absent fruit
stood for their barren hearts. He cursed
not me, not them, but
(ears that hear not, eyes that see not)
their dullness, that withholds
gifts unimagined.

DENISE LEVERTOV

Five

·····································

Developing the Poetic Voice

Shaped by Prayer & Contemplation

The poet does not see and then begin
to search for words to say what he sees;
he begins to see and at once begins to say or to sing,
and only in the action of verbalization
does he see further.

DENISE LEVERTOV

My third-grade teacher, Mrs. Mallory, was a great lover of literature, especially poetry. She taught our elementary school class how to write using the simpler poetic forms—couplets, haikus, limericks. And the more this remarkable woman delighted in our childish scrawls, the more furiously I scribbled them onto my Big Chief tablet.

I learned to relish the formidable challenge of squeezing in the *exact* amount of syllables to make the rhyme sound just right—like a rhythmic drum cadence. And there were no steel, chain-link fences around my poetic playground either. I wielded those fun word crayons like pretend scabbards, scribbling my way outside the lines and over the moated castle walls of respectable grade-school behavior.

That's how poetry became my scrapbook, a literal, written chronicle of my life's history from age eight to eighteen. Sometimes when pictures aren't enough to portray my most important interior moments, there are the poems—hundreds of them. They rise up to speak to me from paisley-fabric-covered blank books; from wild, mod, seventies-print spiral notebooks; from blue, scalloped-edge stationery.

When I first began dating my husband, he thumbed through each of those pages of my life, glancing through my history in word pictures. Suddenly it was as if Scotty had lived with me forever through all of those rites of passage: my happiness at my sister's birth, my heartbreak over my high school romance. He also read as I struggled to describe my first encounter with this strange, new, wonderful Jesus. And yet even when poetry fell short, it communicated perfectly: poetry was only a reflection of the source and not the Source itself.

Poetry later became my comforter. During college it was my braille in a sightless world—the way my heart's fingertips saw, felt, scanned, interpreted my way through a difficult year of death, illness and broken dreams. When I felt unable to pray, my poems were my prayers. I received few answers during that difficult time. Yet through the lasting miracle of language, I can now see how my soul wept and mourned and clawed its way into believing the truth about those invisible, everlasting arms. As was true in the Old Testament story, words and images now serve as my memorial, my rock pile of Ebenezer stones—my tangible heap of evidence that God never leaves us, even when it is difficult to believe he is there.

As an adult, I worked as a writer for various organizations. Then poetry suddenly zigzagged me into a different world. I began to take poetry seriously—not as a hobby, but as a calling. As opportunities arose, I attended free poetry readings, developed relationships with friendly fellow poets, participated in creative writing workshops. And somehow over the years the organic connection between Christ and poetry crept, spread, became inextricably intertwined with my soul.

While pursuing my master's degree in biblical counseling, I studied under a professor who had a special interest in narrative theology. His creative approach inspired me to further explore the connections between Scripture and story, between poetry and spiritual growth. And I soon discovered that the more I studied the Bible, the more poetry permeated the way I viewed my faith.

Poetry has now become my everyday language, my means of expressing what I see, how I feel. Yet what I enjoy most about poetry is really the simplest thing of all: it gives me a way to speak the love of God into my world. Poetry has given me a voice.

The Importance of Voice

The literary skill of persona or *voice* is the poet's own unique style of saying something. It is the poetic characteristic that enables us to say of a work, "That is an Eliot poem" or "That is clearly the work of Yeats."[1] A strong voice—an unforgettable manner of seeing and speaking that is unique to an individual poet—is an almost indefinable and unteachable element of good poetry. Yet it is incredibly necessary.

Take, for example, Allen Ginsberg's controversial poem "Howl." A landmark work when it was published decades ago, this protest poem wails verse after verse of vulgar yet prophetic horror. Whatever we might think of the subject matter, Ginsberg's poem is nonetheless a good demonstration of this element of poetic voice. We're immediately struck by its strong sense of persona: through the power of voice, Ginsberg grabs our souls by the throat and refuses to let go. Yet developing such a distinct voice requires a very specific creative exercise.

Poetry therapist Arthur Lerner recounts a moment when years ago he heard the writer John Ciardi speak at the Breadloaf Writers Conference. Ciardi reminded the gathering that a writer's discovery of his or her true voice "is a matter of time, courage, and patience which can only be earned and learned in a solitary way."[2] Although poets eventually discover more and more of their voice in the context of community, their journey toward speaking what is uniquely theirs first begins in private as they spend time writing.

Voice develops as the writer spends time alone with his or her craft.

The Poetry of Prayer

As poets of the soul, we too develop a strong sense of voice when we spend time alone—alone with our God. And as John Ciardi notes about writing, developing our voice—the honesty before God required for him to work authentically and uniquely through our lives—takes time, courage and patience to develop.

When Jesus talks about the poetry of prayer, he describes a creative intimacy that best develops away from the gaze of the crowd. He says that those who pray in public have already received their reward, but that those who pray in secret will be rewarded openly.

"When you come before God," he says, "don't turn that into a theatrical production. . . . All these people making a regular show out of their prayers, hoping for stardom! Do you think God sits in a box seat? Here's what I want you to do: Find a quiet, secluded place so you won't be tempted to role-play before God. Just be there as simply and honestly as you can manage" (Mt 6:5-6 *The Message*).

The passage urges us to pray privately so that we won't be tempted to role-play before God and others—to take on a "false voice." Instead, when we sit down alone with Jesus—speaking to him honestly, listening reflectively—we're simply seeking to know his heart, his voice. And it is through an ever-growing intimacy with the poet heart of God that we further grow in our ability to speak his words of poetry into our fallen world. Christ's voice wondrously and mysteriously becomes woven into our own—and again, his voice, like his image of love, is revealed differently through each one of us. We each have a voice in God's choir—the body of Christ—in order for the music to have its fullest possible expression.

Quiet, intimate prayer requires patience, persistence. We're like opera singers, diligently vocalizing our prayers daily in order to grow our voice, to maintain its pure, clear sound in the world. And without such spiritual exercise it's easy to grow lazy as we live—and voice— our faith in the world. We can grow complacent and begin to imitate the harsh, noisy voices that often dominate God's expression in the world. Those voices can drown out Jesus' true voice—the voice of the tender Shepherd.

Lost and Found

I am wary of truth that cannot be told
*   in a whisper.*
Why truth at twenty decibels?
Sweaty preachers with throbbing carotids,
All hysteria and calisthenics
With no absolution to pronounce.

After all, didn't life begin in a peaceable garden?
Didn't God breathe into Adam?
Didn't He cradle and kiss him into life?
You tell me. You read it, too.
And even if you didn't, you guessed it
*   long ago.*
Dumb as dirt, dumb as a rock.
A nothing
A nobody
Still, you knew.

You saw the lake light rising in the autumn night
On the blowzy, velvet blooms at the farthest edge
*   of water.*

Quiet, mossy paths will take you where you want to go.
In the clearing, see the trembling of light and shadow?
Leaves, easy as liquid, splash and turn
  on silver branches.
There is no intimation of slick forgiveness here.

Your heart batters your bony ribs.
You remember sweaty, hazy nights as a child
When you crouched in the rotting
  well house, hiding
Smelling the gamey stench of dead things
Waiting for the cry Olly, Olly, in free
A fluid stay of execution,
Vast and humane.

JUDITH GILLIS

As the poet says, Christ's redemptive song of "Olly, Olly, in free" is vast, humane. His music of grace is compelling and richly orchestrated, never manipulative or strident. And to hold fast to the truth of his voice, no matter what other voices say, we're called to patiently seek that distinctive music in secret prayer.

That same struggle—seeking other voices to tell us who we are and what to think—exists in the writing world as well. In his classic work *Letters to a Young Poet,* Rainer Maria Rilke addresses a battle common to poets—the compulsion to seek outward affirmation of one's calling to write. When one young poet asked Rilke what he thought of his poems, the elder replied:

> You ask me whether your verses are good. You ask me. You have asked others before. You send them to magazines. You compare them with other poems, and you are disturbed when certain editors reject your efforts. Now (since you have allowed me to advise you) I beg you to give up all that. You are looking outward, and that above all you should not do now. Nobody can counsel and help you, nobody. There

is only one single way. Go into yourself. Search for the reason that bids you write; find out whether it is spreading out its roots in the deepest places of your heart, acknowledge to yourself whether you would have to die if it were denied you to write.[3]

As Rilke says, writers need to look inside their own hearts rather than for the approving voice outside that says, "Write!" Similarly, in the poetry workshop of the soul, prayer helps us find our true voice before God. We don't have to rely on outward voices for approval, as loud or popular as those voices might be. Instead we become acquainted with Christ's voice, and his voice leads us. As Rilke says about writing, we're to find out if Christ's roots are spreading to the deepest places of our hearts—and whether we would die if we could not live for him.

When I think of this development of spiritual voice, I can't help but think of some good friends of ours, John and Gail Wessells. John is a musician, and several years ago he experienced the unique leading of the Spirit's voice through prayer. He felt prompted to visit head-trauma centers—to sing and read Scripture to comatose people.

Such an idea seemed strange to say the least: to spend hour after hour singing to people who show no signs of response, of conscious recognition. Other voices in the Wessells' lives told them such an outreach was a waste of time—that they could be doing more helpful and productive ministry work, such as feeding the homeless. Yet John and Gail persevered in their unique calling.

One day a few years after they began their ministry, something amazing happened: a man named Bob began to respond. Soon he was speaking. While in his vegetative state, he told them, he had heard their songs of praise, their words of hope. Bob had become a Christian while still in his coma.[4]

Yet I know that even if such a dramatic event hadn't taken place, John and Gail would still be singing to the people they've been called to comfort. Through prayer they've discovered the unique voice, the unique song of Christ they're called to sing in the world.

The Poetry of Contemplation

Yet another way we gain our voices as soul poets is through contemplative reading of the Scriptures—*lectio divina*. Again, ironically, we gain our own creative words to speak into the world by knowing God's own words. This is another paradox of living by poetry: Christ says that those who seek to save their lives will lose them, but those who lose their lives for his sake will find them (see Mt 16:25). According to Jesus, we discover our unique voice by abandoning our pursuit of it. Instead, we are to pursue the one who grants individuality, rather than pursue the gift of uniqueness itself. Through our meditating on the Scriptures, God invites every soul poet to lose his or her voice in order to regain it anew, even more creatively and clearly.

Once again the clergyman poet George Herbert comes to mind, because he illustrates this matter of "losing but finding one's voice" so well. His work, though powerfully original, is saturated with allusions to (and even the voice of) the Scriptures. The poet's biographer Izaak Walton remarked of Herbert, "Next [to] God, he loved that which God hath magnified above all things, that is, his Word."[5]

I call Herbert's use of God's Word "biblical re-creation." The Scriptures were so intricately woven into the fabric of his life that certain portions of it in his work come across as original thought.[6] About Herbert's poetry collection *The Temple*, literary critic Chana Bloch writes:

> There is scarcely a poem in Herbert's *Temple*—one might say scarcely a line—that does not refer us to the Bible. . . . We cannot get past the title page of the volume without some knowledge of the Scripture, and readers had better have the Bible at their fingertips . . . if they expect to enjoy Herbert's poetry with anything like its full resonance. As a Protestant and a clergyman, Herbert knew the Bible so intimately, and as a poet used it so extensively, that it will not do to call it an "influence," certainly not just a "literary" influence.[7]

The structure of *The Temple* closely resembles the Psalms in a number of ways. It's a book of pastoral poetry—instructive, meditative and reflective of a devoted shepherd who seeks to encourage his flock.

In writing these poems, Herbert saw himself as just one part of the family of Christian believers (which supplies one meaning of the title, *The Temple*). Herbert believed that what held true for him from the words of Scripture was undoubtedly true for his brothers and sisters as well.[8] So, for him, the act of writing was both an act of community and a contribution to it; he wanted his own spiritual process to connect deeply with that of others.

Yet the individuality of Herbert's poetry isn't stifled by his communal vision. On the contrary, it seems refreshingly liberated. The same is true regarding the influence of the Scriptures on his work. Rather than restricting his poetic liberty, God's Word seemed to open the door to creative freedom for Herbert:

> What we find at the heart of Herbert's poetry is not the spectre of God cornering the sinner into submission, nor, alternatively, that contemporary vision of the spirit freeing itself to untrammeled self-realization, but rather the image of the believer confronting, assimilating, and speaking the Word of God in his human and fallible existence. When "thy words" are made "my words," as so often in *The Temple*, when they are taken off the printed page and admitted to the heart, they do not obliterate the self but rather free it to fulfill its high purpose—as God's own creation.[9]

In Bloch's view, Herbert's love of the Word propels his creative work: "The Bible is not constricting but enabling for Herbert, opening the 'closets' of the heart, freeing him to speak more fully, more truthfully, than he might otherwise have done."[10]

As Herbert's poetic voice connected him to God, this process benefited his own personal growth, including the development of his voice. And at the same time it also encouraged the church. In short, this poet lost his voice in reverence to something larger than himself, only to regain it as his own, one-of-a-kind voice.

As we see in the poetry of George Herbert, contemplating the Scriptures, mulling them over in our hearts and minds, can allow us more room than we ever dreamed possible. It's how we get to know

God's heart. It's how we discover the voice he's given us to use for his purposes. Through absorbing the living poetry of the Scriptures, we can lose our own limiting ideas about the ways God can speak through us and gain creative freedom. And that creative freedom always works toward the good of others.

The poet Galway Kinnell remarks in an interview, "If it's really a poem . . . it takes on that strange voice, intensely personal yet common to everyone, in which all rituals are spoken. A poem expresses one's most private feelings; and these turn out to be the feelings of everyone else as well."[11]

Likewise, the genuine voice of faith seeks to express the common feelings of all. Such a voice works for the good of the entire poem—the entire body of Christ. "A body," says Paul, "isn't just a single part blown up into something huge. It's all the different-but-similar parts arranged and functioning together" (1 Cor 12:14 *The Message*). We each are given something to say for the sake of all the other members. We each play a part, as God's poetic voice whispers, shouts and sings through each of us in creative, one-of-a-kind ways. These nu-merous flesh-and-bone expressions of Christ connect us to a single greater good: his larger-bodied purpose in the world.

That larger purpose is truly a mystery. Theodore Roethke says poets must scorn being "mysterious" and instead "be willing to face up to genuine mystery."[12] Real poetry is like that. It is so far beyond us that we can only stand humbled and amazed in the temple of its wonder. Likewise, the marvelous music made by the body of Christ, that separate-yet-one voice, is one such genuine mystery.

In the poetry workshop of the soul, we learn to sing our musical part in prayer. We further exercise our voice as we contemplate God's Word, allowing it to tune us to his purposes. And together, as the gospel choir of Christ, our diverse harmonies accompany his single melody—as we sing with all our hearts to the voiceless in this seeking, dissonant world.

OverFlow!
Out of the abunDance!
abunDance!
AbunDANCE!
DANCE! DANCE!
Out of the abundance of the heart
the Mouth Speaks
The Soul Peaks
The Heart Swells
The Tongue Tells!

Nadine Mozon

Aberrations of Our Life Poetry

The subjects of the past three chapters—image, rhythm and voice—have explored the soul poet's purpose: we are Christ's poem, an expression of his heart and mind, saved by grace from a destiny of disjointed ramblings. We are poems hoping to be saturated with God's image, rhythmically attuned to the hope of his eternity, and faithfully discovering our voice in order to offer something for the common good.

So what happens when some of these poetic elements are neglected in our spiritual lives? Can we become an aberration of God's poetry by fabricating our own styles, tones and meanings? Can we actually lapse into artistic apathy rather than reflect his beauty and truth? Both art and Scripture suggest that we can and often do.

Sometimes such aberration presents itself in uniformity. For instance, a group of us can begin to look and sound just like one another and in the process lose our uniqueness—individually and communally—to a nonpoetic group mentality. (Think *Stepford Wives* with a biblical twist. Much scarier than the movie!) Whenever such uniformity of "being"—an unvarying use of language, of thought, of expression—permeates a group, it's probably time for some honest, objective poetry criticism from the outside. Is it possible that the Poet's voice, image, rhythm have been obscured?

We can also conceal the Poet's glory when we choose to live as separatists, focusing on what sets us apart from the world around us. There is a spiritual parallel to this sort of poetic "specialist," as Wendell Berry calls it. The result is a protective, self-serving faith. Such a poet, Berry says,

> has made virtually a religion of his art, a religion based not on what he has in common with other people, but on what he does that sets him apart from them. For a poet who believes this way, a poem is not a point of clarification or connection between himself and the world on the one hand and between himself and the reader on the other, nor is it an adventure into any reality or mystery outside himself. It is a seeking of self in words, the making of a word-world in which the word-self may be at home.[13]

What Berry notes about poetry here holds true for our poetic faith as well. Our life poetry isn't meant to be a hideaway where we seclude ourselves from the culture. On the contrary, our humanity creates a common world between us and them, whoever "they" might be. Our faith, as Berry says of poetry, is a venture into a reality and mystery beyond ourselves, beyond our comfort zones. It's always sending us outward to enter the adventure of what is different, unfamiliar.

Sometimes our life poetry's aberration is as simple as this: our faith parades as spiritual doggerel—poorly crafted, sentimental, predictable poetry. Same old tired political speeches; same old patronizing ministry tactics. And people have good reason for not responding to something so superficial. You see, we've been made—and are being *re*made— into an image of beauty (even if our culture doesn't acknowledge the Poet as that beauty's source). So why should we be surprised then when others read—and reject—blurred, distorted images; jarring, jagged rhythms; weak or obnoxious or noncreative voices? In the poetry workshop of the soul, we can always learn from our culture's response to how we dance to the heartbeat of redemption.

As for now, we'll let the image, rhythm and voice of our Poet carry us into the next chapter: the poetry workshop of his church.

Six

Community as Soul Critics

The Poetry Workshop of the Church

Poetry does not change the world,
it changes the poet.

RICHARD EBERHART

I once enrolled in a poetry workshop in New York City that was taught by a widely respected older poet. One evening a fragile-looking woman in our group read us a poem she had written. Midway through her reading, the looks on the faces of the other participants said it all: the poem was just plain bad. It was cliché-ridden, full of grammatical problems, and rambled incoherently about several disparate subjects. My class members shifted uneasily in their seats.

The teacher's response was something I've never forgotten.

Before saying anything else he recited back to her a single line from the poem. I recognized it as the one line that held some element of intrigue. Then he told her, "That line is your poem, and it is a beautiful one. The rest of what you've written doesn't fit with such an articulate, wonderful line. I would begin with this line, and hone it, and see that the next line that follows it is just as good as that one."

That night the woman left our workshop smiling. She was filled with the belief that she had a poem to write, that she had something worthwhile to say. And our teacher hadn't deceitfully flattered her. On the contrary, his wisdom had transformed her. She left both encouraged and challenged, with an invaluable truth: although the poem she'd written fell far short of its intended artistic aim, it was worthy of further work—and it needed that work to achieve its aim.

Galway Kinnell says, "What someone who teaches a workshop mainly does is recognize the passages that are alive and true and show those to the author."[1] This holds true for all of us who participate in the poetry workshop of the soul. Like my wise workshop leader, God is at work uncovering those parts of our hearts that are most alive to him. He both encourages us in our beautiful life-lines and points out our doggerel-digressions. And as is true in every poetry workshop, this work often occurs in community. He uses our fellow participants in the poetry workshop of the soul—the members of the body of Christ.

The Church as Poetry Workshop
Whenever you enter any writing workshop, you immediately notice that some participants are shy beginners, others confident veterans. There are timid whisperers who barely squeak out their poems when they read. And there are others who stand tall and brazen and read with bravado. The atmospheric pressure of the workshop may be filled simultaneously with gray clouds of intimidation and brisk breezes of confidence. That's because every poetry workshop is a chaotic, colorful mix of methods, styles and voices, of bruised egos and bursting hearts, of polka dots, stripes and plaids.

Just like the church.

In the poetry workshop of the church, the historically rooted, ritual-loving, sonnetlike Episcopalians may gaze uneasily at the fuchsia-draped, gold-earringed, free-verse Pentecostals. At the same time the complex, epic Greek Orthodox soul poets might actually find a lot in common with the simple, haiku contemplatives. Meanwhile, the weepy, "Footprints"-loving members may infuriate those of the obtuse, T. S. Eliot "Hollow Men" persuasion. All are human, gorgeous, flawed, divine. All are different. And all need each other.

The poetry workshop of the church necessarily broadens our idea of community. It offers us a set of binoculars for the heart by giving us a sort of bird's-eye view into human behavior. As we sit next to our fellow poems/poets around the workshop table, we begin to recognize that even the newest or strangest members in our circle have much to offer us. Every voice, no matter how different from ours, is an important one. And because the body of Christ is a huge, organic form that continually grows, expands and changes, the Ephesians passage "we are his *poiēma*" truly means a free flow of community.

When we participate in the poetry workshop of the soul, we're invited to become works in progress that fit together in the poetry collection that is the larger body of Christ. Every encounter with a fellow poem/poet is an opportunity to reflect the glory of our Poet-Creator as we grow, change and learn. It doesn't matter whether we sit next to precise Presbyterians during Sunday services or get down to Bible-study business at the doughnut shop with our Baptist friends on Monday morning. As we converse with different poetic styles, our own poetry ripens into a broader, more meaningful expression of faith.

Within this large body of believers, however, we all need intimate fellow poets who will workshop with us more intently. We need those who more closely observe our life's poetry—those who, as Galway Kinnell says, will recognize what is "most alive and true" in our souls. We need those who will challenge us when our hearts become disengaged and our life poetry digresses into the writer's taboo of cliché: easy, cheap sentimentality and rote recitations of our beliefs. We each need fellow poems/poets who will intuit deeply our unique spiritual rhythm, image and voice, and will not hesitate to comment on them.

In short, we all need not just poetry friends but poetry critics. And if we're to be good poets, we'll participate in the life poetry of those we love and workshop with.

What Makes a Good Poetry Critic?

In his collection of essays *The Sacred Wood*, T. S. Eliot discusses the important role of criticism in English literature. First, he says, every successful critic possesses "interest in his subject, and ability to communicate an interest in it." The good critic also "is the person who is absorbed in the present problems of art, and who wishes to bring the forces of the past to bear upon the solution of these problems."[2]

These characteristics of a critic apply equally to our work in the poetry workshop of the church. The good critic here is someone who is deeply interested in our lives—who is willing to bring all of his or her gifts to the workshop table to help us improve our life poetry. He or she is simply someone who cares about what we're writing. And if we are to be good critics as well, we're called to care deeply for the life poetry of the few we workshop with.

Eliot further points out that good criticism comes from those who fully live out an artistic calling themselves: "The artist is—each within his own limitations—oftenest to be depended upon as a critic; his criticism will be criticism, and not the satisfaction of a suppressed creative wish—which in most other persons, is apt to interfere fatally."[3]

Good criticism, as Eliot says, requires living out the creative wish simultaneously. This is also true in our own poetic soul process. To be an effective critic, we must creatively live out our own faith calling. Too many times our criticisms in the church stem from guilt, regrets or jealousies. Yet our observations of others need to emerge from passionately living our own spiritual creative wish. That is the best gift we can offer others.

As Galway Kinnell says, true critics know their real work is found in spotting the soul's bright blooms of color—the parts that are most alive with God's presence. That is how good poetry—and poetry of the soul—gets written.

Blessing

When light has abandoned the morning
and wind beats the trees into tatters,
when enough rain falls to tell you
that God is again flooding earth,
when all day you burrow in books and learn
only that genius exists, but you don't have it,
when finally everything's drowned
except you and your tedious pride,
then how startling to open your door to umbrellas
blossoming yellow and red in the hallway.

JUDITH TERRY McCUNE

Good critics in the poetry workshop of the soul are also respectful of their fellow pilgrims' life poetry. We see this kind of intimate care illustrated in a story that poet Marvin Bell tells about Allen Ginsberg. The two were taking a stroll when a young poet they knew approached them. The young man asked Ginsberg, "What do you think of Creeley's new book?" His tone was evident—he obviously didn't like Robert Creeley's work. Ginsberg's reply to him was simple and direct: "Whatever Bob's doing, I'm *for* him."[4]

That's the mark of good critics. No matter what you might be writing with your life, or how badly you're writing it, good soul critics are *for you*. They want to see the poetry of your soul flourish, grow, change—surpass their own. They long to see you become all you can be for the sake of God's kingdom.

I have a handful of such soul critics who know my life poetry intimately. A certain good friend often names the nuances of my vocal inflections. "You sound wistful today," she says. Or, "You sound irritated." My friend notices how God's life is either blooming or withering within me, and in her kind yet knowing way, she won't hesitate to point out either. I hope she would say the same of me. We are deeply committed to seeing each other grow as soul poets.

Poetic Forms

The poet Mary Oliver notes, "The best thing about workshops is that people learn there they can change, they can write better and differently from what they had always thought themselves capable of, and this is so often the good news they have been waiting for that all the perils are small beside it."[5] The poetry workshop of the soul is a place where we can not only face our fears but also earn our wings.

One joy that occurs in a good workshop is that members have the opportunity to trace each other's progression and growth. Each member knows where a particular poet began his or her writing of a poem. And as the workshop continues, each can see the others' poetic growth—in the colorful painting of an image or in the growing power of rhythm. The same is true of our own creative process of spiritual growth: as we workshop together with others, we share the joy of seeing one another's life poetry blossom and grow.

We've seen in the three previous chapters how helpful it is for soul poets to know the basic elements of poetry: image, rhythm and voice. But there's more: in the poetry workshop of the church, the poet can also grow by studying and enjoying God's use of various forms of poetry.

There's a wide variety of poetry forms, perhaps hundreds of forms in all. Why so many? The particular form a poem takes allows the poet to express the content of the poem more meaningfully. As such, form becomes one of the poet's most valued tools. The poet Robert Creeley declares, "Form is never more than an extension of content."[6] The substance or meaning of a poem is its content; form is merely the *vehicle* for that content.

Likewise, in our life poetry God's Spirit within us is the content—

and our various forms of expressing his Spirit are just human vehicles for that content. Poets choose particular forms to achieve different ways of expressing their messages. In the poetry workshop of the soul, our Creator-Poet designs various expressions of himself for different reasons.

For the purposes of this book, I'm calling these differing human expressions his poetic "forms." Of course, no person can be defined by any one poetic form—or any other label, for that matter. Yet I've discovered there truly are uncanny resemblances between certain types of people and certain poetic forms.

So here's a short list of some common poetic forms I've encountered in the poetry workshop of the church.

Sonnet

The sonnet is a highly structured, fourteen-line poem that has a definite rhyme scheme. There are several types of sonnets, but probably the most familiar is the Shakespearean sonnet. It has a line-to-line rhyme scheme of *abab, cdcd, efef, gg*. The Petrarchan sonnet, on the other hand, is composed of an octave (eight lines) of *abbaabba*, followed by a sestet (six lines) of any number of combinations, such as *cdcdcd, cdecde, cdccde* or *cdccdc*.[7]

A sonnet is essentially a complete thought in poetic form. In other words, when poets choose a sonnet as their form, they're indicating a desire to express a fully rounded thought. A sonnet is never essentially a question or plea; it's an idea that evolves to completion by the final line of the poem.[8] The poet Denise Levertov says of this structure, "A sonnet may end with a question, but its essential structure arrives at *resolution*."[9]

The following well-known sonnet by Shakespeare illustrates this:

XXIX

When in disgrace with fortune and men's eyes,
I all alone beweep my outcast state,

And trouble deaf Heaven with my bootless cries,
And look upon myself, and curse my fate,
Wishing me like to one more rich in hope,
Featur'd like him, like him with friends possess'd,
Desiring this man's art, and that man's scope,
With what I most enjoy contented least;
Yet in these thoughts myself almost despising,
Haply I think on thee,—and then my state,
(Like to the lark at the break of day arising
From sullen earth) sings hymns at heaven's gate;
*   For thy sweet love remember'd such wealth brings,*
*   That then I scorn to change my state with kings'.*

WILLIAM SHAKESPEARE

Throughout the poem the writer wrestles with his ongoing despair. But beginning with the ninth line, he suddenly resolves his conflict by thinking about "thy sweet love." Suddenly all is reconciled, and he is at peace.

In the poetry workshop of the church, the human "sonnets" relish resolution also: order, symmetry, closure. They may enjoy regular Bible studies, carry neat Daytimers, clean their kitchen floors once a day. They often possess extraordinary gifts of organization and administration. For such people, beauty is found in the fine details. They derive great satisfaction from anything that brings completion—a list of business projects finished, a dirty garage tackled, a relational problem resolved.

When I think of how sonnets often express their faith, I think of how consistently one of my mentors led our study group through a two-year, verse-by-verse exploration of the book of Philippians. I think of systematic theologians, who help unclog the drainpipes of our beliefs, flushing out the residue of rote religion and allowing the clean water of pure faith to flow freely.

Yet sonnets' desire for the beauty of order sometimes leads to unrealistic expectations of themselves and others. Sonnets often insist that their private world line up in perfect harmony. Sonnets tend to approach the Bible strictly as a guidebook rather than as a living story that emancipates them to live more creatively and freely.

I see sonnetlike thinking in the writings of the apostle Paul, as he carefully builds case after case in defense of the faith. His highly structured arguments, embedded in his warm, pastoral epistles, reflect a depth of order and careful thinking. There is crisp logic in Paul's writings. Yet we also see in his epistles a frank willingness to record what is confusing and human—his verbal brawl with Peter, for example.

Sonnets soar higher and sing clearer when they don't just adhere to a form but fully live out the heart of the form. They can move more fluidly, easily, humanly through their everyday lives when structure is no longer their ultimate goal. As they focus instead on the life of Christ flowing through their unique sonnet structure, they seem freer to color outside the lines—while still remaining firmly within the bigger picture.

I remember a discussion I once had with a sonnet friend. She likes to spend time in her kitchen, and so our conversation eventually landed on cooking as a metaphor for her life. She knew that for her to bake really good cookies (and to also have fun in the process), she'd need to get more used to messes—to get flour on her face. She wanted to learn to play more in order for her sonnetlike spiritual life to thrive.

The following Vassar Miller poem illustrates a playful take on the sonnet structure. The poem, a true sonnet, moves so effortlessly that we're hardly aware of its highly ordered rhyme scheme:

On Opening One Eye
Dear Lord,
> *forgive me if I do not wake just yet*
although the air unrolls its silk
to ripple in the sunlight wavering through the milk-
gray clouds; although in the lithe grass, all stubby legs,

puppies and kittens tumble, living Easter eggs;
although the morning flows
over my eyelids shut and graceless,
dear Lord, forgive me, if I seek repose
from night, the nurse who, dark and faceless,
lays me on her dry breasts without a song.
I will wake before too long,
and over my lean and Lenten ribs
put on, more delicate than spiders' webs,
dear Lord. Your satin day,
and go my way.

VASSAR MILLER

Just as this poet plays with the sonnet form, sonnets in the poetry workshop of the church are liberated to enjoy their structure as a means to love God and others rather than as an end in itself.

Free Verse

As opposed to the highly structured sonnet, free verse is loose, with no rules or set ways of thinking. It riffs its way through various forms and expressions. It can scatter across the page like flung birdseed, or it can wander down, line after line, like a free-flowing brook. Or it may simply arrive as a brief, elegantly stated image, such as this one:

An Easter Lily
Tonight the sky received
A paschal moon
It came on time
And through half-open shutters

Its ceremonial radiance
Enters our houses
I for my part received
An Easter lily

Whose whiteness
Is past belief

Its blossoms
The shape of trumpets
Are mute as swans

But deep and strong as sweat
Is their feral perfume.

ANNE PORTER

The point of free verse isn't to be utterly autonomous from other forms of poetry. Its point is for each poet to attempt to create his or her own rules, all for the sake of structure.[10]

Ironically, well-written free verse is a difficult task. It relies on unique rhythms and individualized stanza breaks. "The free verse poem establishes a texture without metrical regularity," says Paul Fussell.[11] Since there's no ordered rhyme scheme to follow to achieve that texture, the poet must rely on his own sense of timing and movement. Yet free verse's freedom doesn't necessarily guarantee that the poem will be interesting or engaging: "A free-verse poem without dynamics—without, that is, perceptible interesting movement from one given to another or without significant variations from the same norm established by the texture of the poem—will risk the same sort of dullness as the metered poem which never varies from regularity."[12]

The human free versers I know are the opposite of sonnets. They chafe at fences, restrictions, structure. They roam and ramble through life, doing many things at once. One free verser I know describes herself as a "spiritual Rollerblader"—whizzing in and out of the church's relational traffic, up and down the sidewalks of the Word. Like other free versers I know, she's an erupting volcano of spiritual passion.

Because of that, free versers are sources of great enthusiasm and energy. They ignite others into action. They often are agents of spiritual renewal, as their passion jars others out of spiritual complacency. Free versers bring vitality to the church.

I think of the apostle Peter as a free verser. One minute he swashbuckles a sword to cut off a soldier's ear in defense of Jesus, yet in the next minute he can't even admit to a simple peasant girl that he's Jesus' friend. Peter appears unstable, unreliable. Yet Christ turns our skeptical perception of free verse on its head, telling us that his entire church would be built on this shaky-looking rock. Go figure.

Free versers often consciously need to seek out more structure and form in their lives. They turn to liturgical worship or to the study of church history or to the discipline of spiritual direction. They intuit that without some underlying grid or more focused pattern to their free-verse way of living, their life poetry can digress into dull, meaningless, self-referential verse. Their constant movement will not read as purposeful poetry but as random meanderings. And the very form that seems so freeing can suddenly become restricting. Thoughtful spiritual structure can give their vibrant, vivid life poetry a fuller, richer feel—and further contribute to the vitality they bring to the church.

Haiku

Traditionally a Japanese form, the haiku originated when poets attended parties for the purpose of corporately writing long poems called *renga*. A renga was made up of short stanzas, and poets often made up a stanza or two beforehand, hoping they would be called upon to offer up the first stanza. Since each gathering usually produced only one renga, lots of the poets' starting stanzas, called *hokku*, were never used. Eventually, the poets began publishing these unused verses, naming them "haiku."[13]

Haikus traditionally were short, three-line poems, with a combination of five, seven and five syllables. Today the rules are a bit freer.

Many poets write haiku in three short lines with no syllabic restrictions.[14]

A haiku is generally understood to be a poem that concisely but sensuously records the essence of a moment.[15] Haikus are usually about common, everyday experiences and are written in very simple, direct language. They're considered one of the most intense poetic forms, and their power lies in strong images and brevity of expression. Here is one example:

Bamboo bending low—
Face of moon in lotus pad—
Showing me the way.

BILLIE RUTH HOPKINS-FURUICHI

In the poetry workshop of the church, human haikus value simplicity, meditation, peace. They often take behind-the-scenes roles. Their words are usually few and carefully chosen. They are quiet doers who are drawn to contemplative worship. They remind the rest of us of the important need for spiritual retreat, for the simplifying of busy lives.

Contrary to what some might think, it is often more difficult to write a good haiku than it is to produce a poem in a longer form. Loading intense imagery and meaning into three lines requires discipline and concision. Similarly, the lives of haikus look deceptively simple—but they pack a punch. Underneath their uncomplicated demeanor usually lie profound depths of meaning. Haikus have something important to say.

The apostle Andrew is a good example of a haiku. He was the quiet brother of Peter who showed up in Jesus' life in some very simple but key ways. For instance, when Andrew overheard John the Baptist saying that Jesus was the Lamb of God, he ran to tell his brother Peter that the Messiah had come (Jn 1:41). The next verse is perhaps most telling about Andrew: "And he brought him to Jesus" (Jn 1:42 NIV). Language equaled quiet action: Andrew was the one who introduced Peter to Christ.

When some visiting Greeks in Jerusalem grew curious about Jesus, guess who was asked to make the introductions. Scripture says the Greeks first asked Philip to meet Christ, but Philip went directly to Andrew. Apparently Andrew was an uncomplicated man who, in some hidden ways, got the job done.

Important things happened through Andrew's simple lifestyle. And important things happen through haikus. To grow poetically, however, haikus recognize their need to take uncomfortable risks in complicated territories. Their bent toward contemplation can often be a convenient withdrawal from the messy business of relationships. And they're often prone to disdain the lifestyles of, say, free versers, thinking those forms should live as unobtrusively as they do.

Yet often these criticisms arise from haikus' fears of living fully—which, in their case, means living out *simplicity* itself with great passion. They're often afraid they have nothing of value to offer the rest of the workshop. Or they can be unaware of the amazing power found in the simplicity of the Image they present to the world. ·

In the poetry workshop of the church, haikus face their insecurities head-on. They learn to appreciate the other poetic forms as much as their own. They embrace the beauty and purposefulness of their own simple, hidden lifestyle without demanding it of others. And just like a haiku poem, their haiku lives pack potent and powerful imagery.

Limerick

A limerick is a rhyming, five-line poem with three beats in lines 1, 2 and 5 and two beats in lines 3 and 4. Although no one is sure how limericks began, it's widely believed that Edward Lear is responsible for making the limerick a vehicle for comedy and nonsense.[16] The familiar rhythm of the limerick seems intrinsically tied to a light-hearted message.

This enjoyable variation of a limerick is by my literarily skeptical brother-in-law, Buzz:

Literature is wonderful, said the old Sage
It stimulates conversation in which to engage
But if you fail to read it
or find you just don't need it
You can use it to line your bird cage.

BUZZ SAWYER

In the church, limericks are the most fun of all. They're happy, jolly good-timers, and they relish laughter and life. They're great comics and they make wonderful storytellers because they naturally see the humor in life situations. To limericks, life is a circus and they're the ringmasters. They point out all the fun underneath the canopy of what they see, and they usually do it quite cleverly.

I once worked for a limerick. He was an editor at a religious magazine, and his absurd sense of humor frequently livened up our workdays. One day our staff received a boxful of clothes that bore Christian slogans. While rummaging through the goods, the editor, a fairly unathletic 250-pound man, pulled out a tiny, extra-small muscle shirt emblazoned with the words "Body by Jesus."

He draped the minuscule shirt over his enormous chest and said, "Hey, I think I'll wear this and go stand outside on the corner as a silent witness for Christ." The mental image he conjured of his protruding torso tightly squeezed into the T-shirt had us all rolling on the floor.

Another longtime limerick friend of ours makes every occasion a laugh fest. Recently he invited us to his home for a sumptuous, five-course meal he prepared. Yet just as wonderful as the meal was the witty repartee he dished out as each course was served. By the time we finished eating, our stomachs hurt both from his fettucine alfredo and our gut-aching, boffo laughter.

The way Elijah interacts with the prophets of Baal seems very limericky (1 Kings 18). As the baleful (or is it "baal-full"?) prophets holler loudly, calling on their god over and over with no response, Elijah gets downright frisky. He starts poking fun at their vain attempts: "Hey, guys, where's your powerful god? Sleeping? Busy? On the commode?"

Elijah took on a serious predicament and had a rollicking good time. He knew a fun opportunity when he saw one, even though he recognized the seriousness of the situation at hand. But when the time came to get down to business, Elijah loudly proclaimed the bald truth of the God of Israel with a sword in his hand. His punch-drunk side gave way to sobriety.

Limericks are more than just fun. They think deeply and meaningfully about life and people. They are courageously committed to God. And they often remind the rest of the workshop of the delight and pleasure found in the dance of redemption. Their enjoyment of life reflects to the rest of us the goodness of God.

Yet sometimes limericks' sense of humor operates as a way to keep people at a distance and protect themselves from pain. It often takes great courage and perseverance for them to allow their emotional depth to surface and for their hearts to be exposed to others.

Other poetic forms are sorely tempted to see limericks solely as comics. It's easy to neglect probing beyond the surface of their gift of laughter. But, paradoxically, when limericks do choose to speak more seriously, their words count. In fact, they have a double impact, because we often listen more carefully to a limerick than, say, to a sonnet (who, like Paul, can be serious nearly all the time). The gift of humor, even in the midst of very serious matters, is a good gift indeed.

In the poetry workshop of the church, limericks grow spiritually by daring to expose deeper parts of themselves to others, by desiring to give people more than a good laugh. At the same time, they can take seriously a true calling—the heart gift of joy they offer the rest of the workshop.

Epic

The epic is one of the most difficult, complicated forms of poetry. The word epic derives from the Greek word epos, of which one meaning is "story." An epic is a long narrative poem that describes the exploits of a heroic individual. One example of an epic is Homer's *Iliad*.[17] "The epic poem is meant to enhance the reader's sense of good and evil," says one writer. The protagonists of epics exist as symbols of "strength, virtue, and courage in the face of conflict."[18]

Even though the hallmark of an epic is its length, it has another distinguishing mark: it does not recount a hero's entire biography but rather starts in the middle of the story and focuses on an important span of time.[19]

In the poetry workshop of the soul, the epics' distinguishing mark is their complexity. Epics are leaders and pioneers, always forging new ground for the rest of us. They frequently face a variety of challenges and battles. Their life stories are often difficult, filled with a wide range of strange twists and turns. If poems were houses, the epic would be a castle with hundreds of mysterious rooms.

One of the epics I know forever regales me with interesting and entertaining stories about her family. Sometimes a single, simple image clues me in to the complexity of the situation she's describing. During one of our conversations, the only way she could describe her relatives' interactions at a family get-together was to call it "Beirut in the kitchen."

When I think of epics, I'm reminded of the psalmist David. His story, like a Sidney Sheldon novel, has it all: facing down giants, playing harps for kings, dancing in the streets; adultery, murder, rape; rebellious sons, family upheaval, national mayhem. You name it, and it's there.

Yet the complexity of David's life isn't what comes to our minds first about the man. In many churches and traditions David is remembered mainly for one phrase from the Scriptures: he was a man after God's own heart.

Epics are often willing to share parts of their story for the sake of others' growth. Like David, they bare their hearts before all, and we benefit from their life lessons. "The strength of the long poem," says poet Galway Kinnell, "is its capacity to show a development, to show an experience in its stages."[20] In the same way the human epics—because of their visibility—allow us a glimpse into their own growth as they journey through life's joys and struggles.

Yet epics' complicated stories can also form a creative barrier. Epics often feel that in order to be in a relationship they need to be understood completely. They believe no one truly gets inside their castle unless they visit every room. Epics also frequently overlook the necessity of what the simpler forms—such as haikus and limericks—offer them. They often impose their epic form on others, thinking their fellow pilgrims' lives should be as complicated as their own.

Epics benefit from learning not just to appreciate but to *need* other forms for their well-being. And instead of seeking to be understood, they learn that their real quest is to be enjoyed, which is something quite different. One can begin reading an epic poem almost anywhere in the text and still savor its language and catch the nuances of the story.

Through their own stories epics can consciously remind themselves and others that, despite all their complicated mountains and valleys, our souls thirst most for a very simple truth—to be a man or woman after God's own heart.

Sonnets, free verse, haikus, limericks, epics. Again, I realize my take on these poetic people-forms offers only a small taste of the smorgasbord of human nature. But you can see where we're headed: the poetry workshop of the church is incredibly diverse.

The Revision Process

Poetry workshops usually include roundtable discussions that focus on a poet's ongoing revision of his or her work. Members are present week after week to encourage each other as they work diligently to hone, shape, sharpen, tighten or expand their poetry. For each participant this process of revision involves listening carefully to learn and know one's fellow poets' voices. For all of us in the poetry workshop of the church, this means being attuned to the variety of ways Christ expresses himself through each of us.

It is also an exercise in creative restraint. One of the most important lessons a soul poet learns when workshopping another's poem is not to impose his or her own form or structure on someone else's work. A delicate sonnet is not meant to be brash, confessional free verse. A simple haiku doesn't need to turn into a complicated epic. Ultimately the purpose of the poetry workshop is for everyone involved to see his or her poetry enhanced and improved from its original form. It's a process of constant revision that allows each life poem to say even better what the Poet intends it to say.

Form is not a cause but an *effect,* says poet Hayden Carruth: "Do we work from the form toward the poem? . . . No, we work from the thing always, from the perception or experience of the thing, and we move thence into feelings and ideas and other cultural associations." In other words, we always work from the inside out, not the other way around. Carruth adds that form simply happens to be a "by-product" of the poetic process.[21]

Often, however, we become preoccupied with the particular form someone uses to express faith, rather than seeing past the form into the heart and purpose of the poem. Whenever we soul-workshop with someone, our role isn't to try to change his or her life poem into our own favorite form. It's to see that the Poet's intent for the poem is most fully and beautifully expressed.

Our Poet gives us different forms for different purposes. The ways God speaks through your life are not necessarily the ways he speaks through mine. But I can learn to better enjoy and understand the ways he expresses his truth through the gifts and personality he has given you for his work.

Even so, the fact remains that major revisions are needed in all of us. There are times in all our lives when our particular form of living just doesn't fit with the poetry we're writing. We may be composing limericks with our lives when our souls are crushed and in need of pouring out free verses of grief. Or we may insist on telling our life tale as an epic, when a haiku version would do. In such moments our community can help us make the revisions we need.

Once you're acquainted with a poet's work, it's easier to know where he or she is hedging, holding back, elaborating too much, relying on tired religious clichés rather than on yielding to the creative power of the image of Christ. This sort of soul work requires that we dive headlong into the business of love, not holding back anything from those who have asked us to participate in their life's revision process.

Revision

If I could erase my life's words
& write over their faint images;
if I could make letters join
curving to form words
that would break hearts & all
that keeps us bound;
if I myself were a word unbound
& binding; if all the letters
of my being could unravel & reknit
into syllables as fresh as rain:

My undoing would be your doing, spell-
binding Word. Making yourself utterable,
you find lost filaments of sound,
mend what is unsound, compose
broken into utterly new.

Primal phonemes, pried
from my deepest parts, surface
rusty, with low groans. I am in agony
to be respoken, rekindled, written

urgently on whatever comes to hand,
a scrap of paper, a wall, or your palm
the way a young girl writes a number
she has no intention of forgetting.

RUTH GORING

What Is Poetic Community?

Perhaps many of our divisions in the body of Christ come from our unyielding adherence to the idea that certain life-poetry forms are better than others. As we learn to appreciate the structured sonnets, the freewheeling free versers, the hidden haikus, the laughing limericks, the expansive epics—and the countless other forms of life poetry—we are free to enjoy each as part of a needed whole. And soon we appreciate more deeply their vibrant poetic role that makes up the wildly varied community of the church.

The Scottish philosopher John Macmurray makes an interesting distinction between a society and a community. He says a society functions around a common purpose that has its members' particular interests at heart. The members are functional, and they cooperate in order to achieve their individual goals. A community, however, is a fellowship, a unity of people. It is not defined in functional terms, and it is maintained not by organization but by mutual affection. It exists solely out of friendship. Its link is the love of its members, free from ulterior purposes.[22]

When I included the word *community* in the title of this chapter, I had this definition in mind. In the poetry workshop of the church, the love given requires us to see that others flourish spiritually, even if their soul poetry looks radically different from ours. It involves remembering that the true poetry of community occurs out of simple love rather than common ideological goals, however noble those goals might be.

This creative love for one another can enable us to even more fully enjoy our poetic differences, our varied expressions of faith. Our favorite poetry "forms"—denominations, lifestyles, personal tastes—are not meant to divide us but rather to bring color into our lives. They are meant to blend us as Christ's vivid expression on the palette of this world.

Leland Ryken says that "the poetic idiom is the poet's way of counteracting the principle that familiarity breeds contempt and indifference."[23] When we give voice to our faith, using the unique words and the poetic form we've been given to express within the body of Christ, we rescue faith from boring overfamiliarity. We dislocate the truth, as T. S. Eliot says, into fresh meaning.

As God's living poetry, we are each a different poem with our own very particular form and style. We each long to be lovingly read, crafted, released to say the things that are most important to us—and him—for the sake of loving others. We are bursting with alive, creative possibility. We are long-suffering works of art, hoping to offer good gifts to one another and to receive goodness and redemption as well.

Welcome to the poetry workshop of the church.

Seven

··

The Blessing
of Brokenness

"Our Common, Puddled Substance"

A poem is a "laying on of hands."

RICHARD EBERHART

Like the often-messy matters of the heart, the calling of writing—
particularly creating poetry—isn't very glamorous. My husband and I
are both freelance writers, and our computers are located in our mil-
dewed basement, right next to the cat litter boxes. More often than
not, the poems I write begin in my head while I'm doing something
ordinary—like standing in the express line at the grocery store to buy
skim milk and toilet paper. Sometimes they are even prompted by
tabloid headlines.

Some people imagine poets enjoying a quiet, beatific life, sitting
cross-legged next to a gurgling stream, writing their verses in red
plaid journals. Yet often that's not possible (since poets also need to
eat regularly, even if it's peanut butter and crackers). Writing poetry is

more frequently an act of pure pleasure, or simple obedience to the call of writing, but rarely, if ever, a means to make a living.

Many poets—even well-known ones—work ordinary, nine-to-five jobs and then do their verse work at night. I think of Wallace Stevens, who sold insurance for fifty years at the Hartford Accident and Indemnity Company. Or William Carlos Williams, who attended to squalling, feverish babies in his family medical practice in Paterson, New Jersey.

Williams actually thought of his daily work as an integral part of his poetry: "It's the humdrum, day-in, day-out, everyday work that is the real satisfaction of the practice of medicine," he writes. "That is why as a writer I have never felt that medicine interfered with me but rather that it was my very food and drink, the very thing which made it possible for me to write."[1]

Then there are the poets who teach the craft of poetry for a living, immersing themselves in others' work as a means to support themselves, to encourage others and to keep their critical faculties sharpened. However, even the joy of teaching poetry can have its creative drawbacks. One poet-professor, Galway Kinnell, says, "The worst thing about teaching is that it puts you in contact mainly with people preoccupied by the things that preoccupy you. It would be better to find a work by which you could enter a world different from your own, in its people, material, and terminology."[2]

Some poets do just this, unearthing ways to remain connected to the raw, real world. I've discovered that my work as a counselor, for instance, requires me to keep my vision—and hopefully my poetry—grounded in the dirt of common life. My daily ventures into other people's lives help keep my heart and hands and feet muddy, as I continually wade into human joy and shame.

Hearing cigarette-butt, broken-beer-bottle stories of unwanted pregnancies and debilitating illnesses and splintered marriages reminds me that, like poetry, real spiritual growth is not a lofty venture. It's about the cracked sidewalks in our hearts, and the semi-strangled but fully alive and gorgeous flowers that mysteriously grow between those cracks. We write the poetry of our lives in a flailing, pain-gulping universe that's drowning in decay. This is, the poet Geoffrey Hill says, "our common, puddled substance."

Fishing for More than Bait

"One does not become enlightened
by imagining figures of light
but by making the darkness conscious."
C. G. Jung

Last night I dreamed
of blue waters
ringed by arches
and walls of transparent glass,
of a swimmer stranded
far from shore.

I dove   down   down   into the depths,
my hand grazing a beautiful orange fish.

Some dreams are numinous shapes
that hover just outside consciousness
like a poem
beginning to unfold in my body,
where I must sit,   blind and alert,
until words form
out of the fecund crepuscular depths
and make their appearance
on the page.

The dreamer's, the poet's task
is this:
to relish the art of fishing,
of casting a line,   to invite the dark shape

in the flickering stream
to bite,
reeling in that visceral tug,
that persistent throb
or inaudible movement
with such excruciating tenderness
that sometimes an image for unnameable truth
comes dripping into the light,
heaving and squirming with life,
gilled in silver,
ready to be tried by fire.

GRETCHEN SOUSA

"Only Stand and Wait"

I know a woman who used to experience overwhelming guilt whenever she couldn't spend at least one hour a day praying. Her guilt was so intense that, if she missed her time one day, she would pray twice as long the next. When I met her, she was contemplating whether even an hour was enough, given Paul's admonition to "pray without ceasing."

As we talked about her compulsion for her daily quiet time, I asked her what she thought would happen if, for some reason, she became mentally incapacitated and could no longer pray or read as a result. She thought for a long time before she answered. "To be honest," she said, "I'd feel I was slipping away from God." We both sat sadly and silently in the dark weight of her statement. For her, connection with God meant relying only on her attempts at relationship with him, not on his toward her.

Over the years we've talked about lots of things, but she says that what means the most to her is a poem I gave her.

John Milton once faced an intense soul-struggle. He was going blind, and he realized he would no longer be able to serve God through his writing. In his desperation Milton wrote the poem "On

His Blindness." And in the process of creating the work, he stumbled on a new meaning of fruitfulness:

When I consider how my light is spent
Ere half my days in this dark world and wide,
And that one talent which is death to hide
Lodged with me useless, though my soul more bent
To serve therewith my Maker, and present
My true account, lest He returning chide,
"Doth God exact day-labor, light denied?"
I fondly ask. But Patience, to prevent
That murmur, soon replies, "God doth not need
Either man's work or his own gifts. Who best
Bear His mild yoke, they serve Him best. His state
Is kingly; thousands at His bidding speed,
And post o'er land and ocean without rest;
They also serve who only stand and wait."

In his darkest hour Milton glimpsed one of God's brightest truths: "This is the *work* of God, that you believe in him whom He has sent" (Jn 6:29 NASB, emphasis mine). The poet eased his aching soul onto the cushions of this restful place. He saw that the work of God is accomplished, first and foremost, in restful trust in the person of Christ—not in what he will do for us, nor in what we do for him, but simply in *himself.*

In the kingdom of Christ's grace, no one is measured by amounts of work or by dispensation of gifts, but rather by love. Those like Milton who can only stand and wait for a better day also serve on bended knee. The heart that can "only stand and wait" is a heart of true faith—one with only the bare, scarred symbol of the cross to cling to. In a modern world that discards the elderly, the mentally ill, the disabled, such a concept is as stunning as the language of poetry. Our culture easily abandons what looks useless. But God doesn't.

Poetry, like our true service to the holy, is many things, but it is not just utilitarian.

Poets and Monks: Nonutilitarian Purpose

Throughout the years philosophers and thinkers have drawn close associations between saints and poets. Even Freud said these are the two classes of human beings who defy all psychological categorizing.[3] The contemporary poet and writer Kathleen Norris has even more fun with the connection. She ironically regards today's monks and poets as "the best degenerates in America," because, she says, both "value image and symbol over utilitarian purpose or the bottom line; they recognize the transformative power hiding in the simplest things."[4]

It's true: monks and poets embrace the power of symbols over usefulness. And Norris's tongue-in-cheek term *degenerates*, says a lot about their approach. The poetic process can be like that of a scavenger. A poet takes the oddest, perhaps even the most despised object in a room, and examines it so thoroughly that light is shed not only on the object but also on the world's condition.

Just as a poet scavenges for objects and images from which to create art, so God sifts and sorts through those parts of our stories that go unnoticed and neglected by us. He finds in the rooms of our souls chipped coffee mugs, old *Life* magazines, broken-down cane-backed chairs—all of which he can use in his transforming process.

The woman I mentioned earlier was suffering deeply, crippled inside. She tells me she served a God of her own making, outside the Scriptures—a false God who required sacrifices, not mercy, a God who demanded endless effort from his people in return for keeping them locked safely inside the gates of his kingdom.

Yet this woman's deep inner conflict was the very tool—the broken chair—that God used to unfold a deeper, richer work in her life. As she began to journal about her spiritual struggle, she discovered a passion for both watercolor painting and poetry writing.

As she ventured into these creative interests, some of the darkest rooms of this woman's spiritual struggles eventually opened a door to blessing. Through her delight in creating art and poetry for her family, friends and neighbors, she could imagine the delight of the Father in his created children. Even though she still struggles with an overactive conscience, she is slowly absorbing God's love and grace toward her—not for her rote religious activities but simply because she's his beloved daughter.

Her new calling—telling her story of faith and redemption through writing and painting—is not of her own creation but of his. Nevertheless, it's risky, uncharted territory for her because it's forged through the tumbleweeds of her soul's terrain.

"Consider your own call, brothers and sisters," Paul says, "not many of you were wise by human standards, not many were powerful, not many were of noble birth. But God chose what is foolish in the world to shame the wise; God chose what is weak in the world to shame the strong; God chose what is low and despised in the world, things that are not, to reduce to nothing things that are, so that no one might boast in the presence of God" (1 Cor 1:26-29).

We all have weaknesses. We all have broken chairs in the living rooms of our souls. And living by poetry involves those broken chairs—our struggles, our thorns in the flesh. Poetry reveals to us that it is the Poet who chooses which object in our living room to focus on, which deeper meaning he will draw from that object, and how that meaning will reverberate into other meanings. In the poetry workshop of the soul, our spiritual growth isn't a creative work entirely of our own making; *he* is the artistic director, the Poet. He knows what poetry to create that will reflect his glory and beauty to the world.

"My strength is made perfect in your weakness," God tells Paul. And as Paul experiences the reality of Christ in the midst of his own limitations, he discovers a strange joy: "So, I will boast all the more gladly of my weaknesses, so that the power of Christ may dwell in me. . . . For whenever I am weak, then I am strong" (2 Cor 12:9-10).

God's consuming desire as our Poet is, essentially, to craft his beauty within us—not for some stark utilitarian use of us, but to reveal something lovely about Christ to our drowning, puddled-substance world. His intent isn't merely to create spiritual success stories or provide definitive answers for our problems, but rather to paint our souls with his nature. And he'll use both bright and dark colors to create his picture. He'll use not only our red-balloon hoots of joy but also our tear-blue cries of weakness to splash Christ across the canvas of our souls.

"We have this treasure in jars of clay," Paul tells us, "to show that this all-surpassing power is from God and not from us" (2 Cor 4:7 NIV). Easier said than done. We like to think God uses the victorious, floating-balloon moments of our lives. It's much harder for us to think he creates out of the weak, deflated ones as well.

Divorced

When Dad divorced us
we were bones discarded,
buried,
flesh bare.
Memories brought him back
resurrecting
the ones with remnant marrow.

In death
he laid down to sleep
with scattered fragments exposed.

I am disinherited:
exploited,
bleaching,
gnawed,
tooth gouged,
forgiving human slight,
waiting a new resurrection
by the true Father.

Derrel Emmerson

Artful Suffering

My favorite poet is a woman named Vassar Miller, who recently passed away. I first discovered her work as I huddled with a poetry anthology in a fusty, cobwebbed corner of a cramped used-book store. I read only one poem, but that was enough. Miller's piercing, sane voice so arrested me that I grabbed a pencil out of my purse, wrote her elegant name on a dog-eared bookmark, and started scavenging bookstores and libraries for more of her works.

By reading a biographical sketch of her, I learned about her life before I had an opportunity to pore over her poetry. She was nominated for a Pulitzer Prize in the early sixties, acclaimed by well-respected poets, treated kindly by ordinarily acerbic critics. Much later, when I finally was able to track down her books, I savored her every word on my tongue like rare fruit. She tasted curious; she tasted strange. But she also tasted incredibly familiar.

A few months later I discovered that Vassar Miller had cerebral palsy. Out of this woman's struggling body erupted the most intense, lovely poetry I'd ever read. I became utterly enchanted by the audacious faith of this woman, who painted delightful pictures of strolls through squishy mud, poked raucous fun at patronizing people, and paid fond tribute to beloved friends.

But I found I was drawn to another side of her poetry as well: Miller struggled against the endless prison of her crippled body. She grieved the absence of romantic love. She adamantly refused to gloss over her own sins or the sins of others against her. She alternately hugged God tightly against her heart and then got downright feisty and fought with him.

I soon realized why I was moved so deeply by her work. I'd tasted vicariously the fruit of her suffering even before I'd learned the painful truth about her disease. There is a generosity of spirit behind her words, words permeated with the rawness of her grief. To me, Vassar Miller not only created suffering's art, but she also embraced *artful suffering*.

If I Had Wheels or Love, Miller's collected work of poetry, includes a poem entitled "For a Spiritual Mentor." Miller writes:

May I not be like those who spit out life
Because they loathe the taste, the smell, the muss
Of happiness mixed with the herb of grief.

I am consistently struck by the paradox that this woman—who seemingly suffered more than a single human ought—would write a poem imploring us not to despise brokenness, "the herb of grief." She had no earthly reason to embrace her pain, but she did—and her suffering was the source of great art. And how she lived her aching life is great art as well.

Artful suffering blazes with poetic beauty because its self-conscious edges are burned cleanly away. It responds to the call to empty oneself, without the self being utterly obliterated. Like Vassar Miller's life and poetry, it fully captures bright Easter days of resurrection and celebration because it has dared to crawl into the dark belly of the earth's wail and lick every salty tear.

Without Ceremony

Except ourselves, we have no other prayer;
Our needs are sores upon our nakedness.
We do not have to name them; we are here.
And You who can make eyes can see no less.
We fall, not on our knees, but on our hearts,
A posture humbler far and more downcast;
While Father Pain instructs us in the arts
Of praying, hunger is the worthiest fast.
We find ourselves where tongues cannot wage war
On silence (farther, mystics never flew)
But on the common wings of what we are,
Borne on the wings of what we bear, toward You,
Oh Word, in whom our wordiness dissolves,
When we have not a prayer except ourselves.

VASSAR MILLER

We live in a world, including our religious world, that despises weakness. Yet the message of the Beatitudes in Matthew 5 creatively contradicts the culture. Jesus says, essentially, the more of God you need, the more of God you'll get. That's not necessarily the way we expect to encounter him. This way of the cross—the way of weakness—is Vassar Miller's subject: "when we have not a prayer except ourselves." When even the words of faith fail us, Christ the Word alone walks toward us, causing our spiritual knock-knees to wobble us straight to himself.

Nothing requires us to need God more than to have all of our spiritual props kicked out from beneath us, and to lie dazed and confused in the straw manger of our soul's true condition. That's why our hearts often seem so ripe for creative growth in the worst possible circumstances—bankruptcy, illness, spiritual failure. Those who struggle deeply are counted as blessed by Jesus if they follow his way, accept his process, open their hearts to the truth of his words alone.

But in order to live by poetry's nonutilitarian concept, something creative is required. We're asked to give up a certain measure of safety, a certainty about what our spiritual lives will eventually look like. Of this poetic safety Rilke writes, "For if we think of this existence of the individual as a larger or smaller room, it appears evident that most people learn to know only a corner of their room, a place by the window, a strip of floor on which they walk up and down. Thus they have a certain security."[5]

If we compare Rilke's statement to our spiritual lives, we can also park our souls on a "strip of the floor" we're familiar with. We don't want to be disturbed by the complexity of life. Yet to open our hearts fully to the Poet means being willing to experience the unpredictable. That includes flinging the doors of our heart open to the Dante's *Inferno* moments of life when they come. We resist living that passionately because it would make us even more vulnerable to the world's sorrow and pain. Yet poets, including poets of the soul, not only describe the world; they also commit themselves to experiencing it in such a way that their own internal reality speaks to the reality in others.

"A poet," Dorothy Sayers wrote, "is [someone] who not only suffers the 'impact of external events' but experiences them . . . [and is someone] with the exceptional power of revealing his experience by expressing it, so that not only he, but we ourselves, recognize that experience as our own."[6]

Many of us immerse ourselves in the world's ways to learn how to manipulate or arrange it for our own security and pleasure. But "the poet knows the world in order to feel it intensely."[7] One writer describes the poet's calling as "a gulf of sorrowing fire [underlying] his rough-wood table."[8] Poets of the soul do not run from that sorrowing fire. Rather, they recognize that the slow waltz of redemptive sorrow can attune us to the heartbeat of suffering in the world around us.

Road out of Kosovo

He trudges along in broken step,
pale face frozen in a blank stare,
and all the long, long river
of moving bodies pass him by.
Even the frail move faster,
framing him against their blur of anguish,
like a film that runs slow motion,
etching one small centerpiece
against the screen of the unwilling eye.

Upon his back—
as if coupled there, ribs fused to ribs—
rides an ancient man, more skeletal
than fleshed,
skull rocking gently, rhythmically,
arms crooked absurdly
over the hard-set slope of shoulders,
hands snatching at the brittle air.
Thin-stick shanks dangle loosely
over the young man's arms,

bob against the plunge and stagger
of his legs—like metronomes
that pace the broken angle of each step,
impeding them.

And still they come, he comes—
this strange, two-headed creature all its own,
with its four unseeing eyes,
its single haunted soul—
like a crab caught in an unremitting tide . . .

an awful metamorphosis,
a horror we cannot look upon,
nor speak of, nor forget.

And still they come, the dying and the young,
inseparable,
like a ghost that rides the shoulders
of the world.

JUDITH DEEM DUPREE

Our common, puddled substance—the broken chairs in our souls —is what helps us better comprehend the nonutilitarian call of the gospel. We follow Christ for the sake of his own raw and very real death, which he offered us as a symbol of his humanity. We follow him in his ultimate brokenness.

Writing from prison, the German theologian Dietrich Bonhoeffer described how that experience had awakened his own sense of humanity: "I often ask myself why a Christian instinct frequently draws me more to the religionless than to the religious, by which I mean not with any intention of evangelizing them, but rather, I might almost say, in 'brotherhood.'"[9]

As he faced death, Bonhoeffer found himself more at home with the human than with the divine. There was no glorying in the high calling, only solidarity with the suffering. Like John Milton in his hour of blindness, Bonhoeffer could only stand and wait. There was no miracle, no miraculous escape, only the bald truth of his plight.

His ultimate sacrifice for the cause of Christ was eventually borne not in an ivory palace of Christian camaraderie but in the lonely, bare stable of shared humanity. The poet Richard Eberhart writes, "It is impossible to conceive of great poetry written without a knowledge of suffering."[10] The poetry of Bonhoeffer's life—and death—echoes these words.

In the poetry workshop of the soul, our most beautiful, stunning lines of poetry can be written in the hour of our greatest weakness.

Thorn in the Flesh

Light comes again
but sometimes
falls at crooked angles.

Now there is song,
but sometimes
the silence conducts it.

My days are full
but sometimes
only of your absence.

I have been healed,
but sometimes
still the whole heart hobbles.

VASSAR MILLER

Eight

···

Living as Sacred Symbols

Poetry & the Prophetic

---

*From your glowing window, look down on
the features of this subtle stake and
recognize the poet—a tumbril of burning reeds
escorted by the unexpectable.*

RENÉ CHAR

I grew up in a small farming community, amid cornflower-blue skies, stiff tumbleweeds and acres of golden, shag-carpet wheat. Our community was a place where moms left their Buick station wagons running when they stopped at the grocery store to get toothpaste. It was a place where after a birth or a funeral or a wedding, friendly faces dropped by with big pots of steaming chili, homemade cornbread and cherry pies—because everyone in town knew everyone else's grief or joy.

In this kind of small community, where everybody's business and reputation were public knowledge, the lifestyle of my party-happy mother was no secret. Although some townspeople wouldn't have necessarily labeled her an alcoholic, most of them did know she was a lively drinker, jazzing up the country club gatherings with her flamboyant presence. In fact, once she sat down at the piano and started playing love songs by ear, you knew she'd be singing until dawn.

One day, however, when I was a young teenager, my mother's life was mysteriously changed. It's a story best told through poetry. I often tell others that whereas Christ's first miracle was to turn water into wine, the first miracle I ever saw was my mother's wine transformed into extravagant living water:

> For this reason I say to you, her sins,
> which are many, have been forgiven, for
> she loves much; but he who is forgiven
> little, loves little.
> Luke 7:47

wine into water
we are emptying the bottles today,
my mother and i,
pouring that amber death down the drain
with unrestrained
hilarity!

did other children know
enemies as fierce
as those glistening glass traps
of poison were to me?

bottles filled with hidden words,
words never heard till she'd
drunk them
and they'd mushroomed inside
like some giant fungus,
foul and deadly,

finally spewing from her mouth:
thick, heavy, blue-violet,
coloring the air with purple rage.

i often peered forlornly
at that liquid held to light,
and wondered if i might strain out those
awful words
and leave just the stinky stuff
for her to drink.

yes, just the words. not her
rollicking laughter,
awakened by gin and ice cubes,
my judy-mom who played the piano
downstairs at daybreak
for slurry-worded lawyers and doctors
while i, liza-legged,
sang along quietly in my bedroom
as she played and wept,
played
and wept
at her rainbow's end.

i think
that's why
they don't understand,
that upper-crust toast of the town
who no longer come to dinner
because my mother now invites
the lame and the blind
and the naked.
they don't understand why
the wretched come in droves
to drink in hope,

gulping down pitchers
of living water
she now pours
with gracious ease.

how the pharisees denounce her,
grimly warn sunday schools of her danger,
remind their children to stay away . . .
but mary magdalene
is my mother
and i believe her,
for she weeps new tears when she tells me,
clear-eyed and sober,
that she has no law but love:

for love has bought her,
won and wooed her, filled her—
and she is now the forever debtor,
spilling herself out
for the one who emptied his all
for her.

"new wine," she tells me,
"not fit for old wineskins."

i wish i could tell them,
those who refuse miracles
as i watch those blue words
and amber death
disappear forever down that drain,

for liquid Love gathers me
in her arms
and squeezes tight, so tight
i bite my lip to contain

orange laughter,

and in my heart
i rehearse
(for the millionth time)
my lines
for the junior high
firing squad:

"all i know is . . .

she who once stumbled
through my life, blind—
now sees . . .

me."

JOY SAWYER

I knew that what had happened to my mother was real, and because of that, I soon believed God was real as well. I could hardly find words to tell my best friends about the amazing transformation I'd witnessed, but I didn't have to. They knew she was different too.

Yet some people responded differently to my mother's startling change of heart. In fact, her conversion wielded a strange sword. Through the polarized reactions to my mom's new life of love and freedom, I first learned that living by poetry is not only lovely but also unsettling. It is not just comforting; it's also prophetic.

The Poet as Prophet

One of the Greek definitions for *prophet* is "poet"—one "who tells the truth." In the Old Testament, poets and prophets were considered one and the same. Their straight-shooting, sorrowful messages began with their own private encounter with God, which they meditated upon and eventually delivered to the people in the form of metrical poetry.[1]

Here is a poetic lament from the prophet Jeremiah, delivered both for himself and for his community:

Although our iniquities testify against us,
act, O LORD, for your name's sake;
our apostasies indeed are many,
and we have sinned against you.
O hope of Israel,
its savior in time of trouble,
why should you be like a stranger in the land,
like a traveler turning aside for the night?
Why should you be like someone confused,
like a mighty warrior who cannot give help?
Yet you, O LORD, are in the midst of us,
and we are called by your name;
do not forsake us! *(Jer 14:7-9)*

The prophet Jeremiah is also the poet Jeremiah, using image, voice and rhythm to deliver God's Word to his people.

Poets and prophets are connected through their shared belief in the evidence of things not seen. The biblical prophets pleaded with Israel to turn away from the visible wood and stone idols they'd fashioned with their own hands and to return to the invisible God, who loved them passionately. In the same way, poets disrupt our culture's idolatry of tangible success and quick-fix answers. They beckon us to discover anew the wonder of spiritual imagination and vision, the invisible matters of the heart, such as hope or love: "The poet-prophet is motivated by his vision of a spiritual life to which others are blind."[2]

That's why the voice of prophetic authority often unsettles us. "The prophet's goal," says one writer, "is to confuse his reader's senses and undermine the operations of his reason, preparing him for the revelation of truths that are unfamiliar or outside daily experience."[3] Poetry has an effect similar to the prophet's words: it "transforms experience and moves the receiver to new attitudes."[4]

In the poetry workshop of the soul, we're given a new prophetic mission. Like the purpose of the Old Testament prophets, our task is to live out God's comforting yet troubling poetry in a prose-benumbed world. As Christ tells us, our very presence as passionate, sacred symbols of God's existence brings not only beauty and hope to the world, but a sword as well.

Yet Christ's sword is not necessarily one of cutting words, moral fury or combative theology. Rather, it is the unmistakable presence of the holy that pricks at our predictable, explainable lives. When the Old Testament prophets delivered the word of God, their message was not popular. It was *Other.* Likewise, today's poets deliver words of life through a means just as unpopular, just as other.

A few years ago the Russian journalist Vladimir Voina wrote a telling article for the *New York Times.* Voina reported that when Nobel Prize-winning poet Joseph Brodsky was invited to speak at a southern university, only a handful of people showed up. After speaking for a few minutes to a nearly empty room, Brodsky turned at one point and said to no one in particular, "Should I continue babbling or end this?" Eventually he stepped down from the podium. No one asked him to continue.

The display of apathy astounded Voina. In his *Times* article he quoted the Russian poet Alexander Pushkin, who compares the role of the poet to that of a biblical prophet "setting people's hearts on fire with the Word." Not many responded then; nor do they now.

It probably shouldn't surprise us that the "otherness" of poetry is not widely embraced. Yet believing in and proclaiming the beauty of poetry is similar to our witness of the redemptive work of the cross: we uphold its value, regardless of how many or few people respond. Like the words of the prophets, poetry's value is not based on the popular response of the people but on the truth of its words.

Jesus

Touching Ezekiel his workman's hand
Kindled the thick and thorny characters;
And seraphim that seemed a thousand eyes,
Flying leopards, wheels and basilisks,
Creatures of power and of judgment, soared
From his finger-point, emblazoning the skies.

Then turning from the book he rose and walked
Among the stones and beasts and flowers of earth;
They turned their muted faces to their Lord,
Their real faces, seen by God alone;
And people moved before him undisguised;
He thrust his speech among them like a sword.

And when a dove came to his hand he knew
That hell was opening behind its wings.
He thanked the messenger and let it go;
Spoke to the dust, the fishes and the twelve
As if they understood him equally,
And told them nothing that they wished to know.

James McAuley

Disrupting the Status Quo

Bible scholar Walter Brueggemann says that the first task of the Old Testament prophet was to cut through a culture's numbness, to penetrate its self-deception. He suggests that one such way was to offer symbols that described the horror causing the culture's numbness and requiring denial. Thus the prophet provided images that disrupted the spiritual status quo.[5]

A writer friend described to me an epiphanic moment he experienced while reading Flannery O'Connor's novel *The Violent Bear It Away*. My friend found himself both fascinated and repelled by the main character, Francis Tarwater—a boy desperately seeking escape from God's call on his life. As my friend pondered his strong reactions to the story of Francis, he was suddenly struck by a disturbing notion: *I am reading about myself,* he thought. *I am running from God too.*

Not long after reading the novel, my friend converted to a life of faith, and he believes Flannery O'Connor is at least partly responsible. "The prophet Flannery told me, 'Thou art the man,'" he said. "Her strange imagery nagged at me until I finally gave in to the God who was pursuing me."

My friend's story is a good illustration of why the callings of novelists and poets correspond with that of prophets: all rely heavily on symbols to communicate their messages. And in his case, those symbols profoundly affected his life. In the same manner, God the Prophet-Poet communicates his message through us, his sacred symbols. Through the power of his living metaphors, he disrupts the spiritual status quo in the world.

The Greek word *metaphoros* means "moving van"—something that "carries over" meaning from one arena of life to another.[6] It is literally, says the poet Delmore Schwartz, "a bearing-across, or a bringing-together of things by means of words."[7]

For example, in Ephesians 5:31-32 the apostle Paul describes the institution of marriage metaphorically. The metaphor of marriage actually "carries over meaning" from the eternal into the earthly: "'For this reason a man will leave his father and mother and be united to his wife, and the two will become one flesh.' This is a profound mystery—but I am talking about Christ and the church" (NIV).

In Paul's description marriage is a "moving van" that transports the reality of God into our everyday lives. The image of a man and a woman bound by covenant love packs up all the household goods of heaven and ferries them into the brand-new home of this world. Through the very earthy image of marriage we experience the symbolism of Christ's eternal relationship with the church.

The power of metaphor is found in its immediate, visceral effect on the reader. Rather than explaining their subjects, metaphors offer a sensual *experience* of the topic being presented. "When the Psalmist writes that his soul thirsts for God (Ps 63:3), he is surrounding his spiritual longing with physical and emotional associations that we experience but cannot adequately put into words."[8] That's why we understand the Psalms as we read them, but we feel them as well.

For example, we can see, feel, hear, even *dance* with the God this poet experiences:

Shadows of God

Where there is Light, shadows spring forth;
they do not distort the Light—only its impediments.

I saw God—
saw Him cradled in a basket, resting to our pliant murmurs, carried gently,
lest He tip and fall before our startled eyes, and scrape His aged, unhuman
skin.

I saw God
hunched down in a mighty go-cart, braced against an empty planet. He set Him
loose with a mighty lurch, raced wildly through the random universe, swerving
past our swiveling souls—sporting with them.

I saw God
marching, marching, hup-hup,
around and down and up our boulevards,
to the thrum and thrall
of martial music trumpeting,
flags a-float and whipping smartly,
white-on-white, against the curved blue sky.
HE stepped out ahead, as large as thunder;
and babes hung onto fathers
who clung closer to their babes—
shivering with thrill and apprehension.

I saw God
grazing in a quiet field—
solid as a bull's broad flank,
made one with trees and toads and field mice
and the steamy excrement we swear by.
He turned, and worked his grassy jaws,
and stared me down;
His tail knew where the flies were.

I saw God—
watched Him spinning—violent dervish—
through the violated air,
catching up our soil and substance,
choking us with all the grit
He'd blown from out our nostrils yesterday,
before He changed His mind and habitat.

I saw God
stand secret watch, wait behind a veil,
the curtain of His cold Fire,
playing Oz within our munchkin minds;
and we—all stiff or floppy—
had set ourselves a-whimpering,
mewling down the endless road toward Him...

I saw GOD, His name,
on tombstones everywhere—
engraved gratuitously, with reverence,
entwined with graceful flora,
with granite vines well-rooted now in Heaven,
or surely meant to climb there—

high enough to touch His golden crown or reach for golden eggs.

JUDITH DEEM DUPREE

Like this poem, which offers us a sensory experience of God, we as living metaphors help others to taste, see, hear, touch, smell Christ: "For we are to God the aroma of Christ among those who are being saved and those who are perishing. To the one we are the smell of death; to the other, the fragrance of life" (2 Cor 2:15-16 NIV). We're invited to provide the world not just with a logical explanation of God but also with *an experience of God*—one that, as we read earlier, undermines the senses and prepares others for new spiritual attitudes.

In a wonderful essay Denise Levertov observes, "We need a poetry not of *direct statement* but of *direct evocation*: a poetry of hieroglyphics, of embodiment, of incarnation."[9] And we need that same fragrant incarnation to permeate our soul poetry as well.

The poet and critic Dana Gioia writes, "By successfully employing the word or image that triggers a particular set of associations, a poem can condense immense amounts of intellectual, sensual, and emotional meaning into a single line or phrase."[10] The power of living as sacred symbols is that we provoke a response. To paraphrase Gioia, God condenses enormous *eternal meaning* into the "single line" of our lives—and we trigger in others eternal (yet personal) associations that let others know he's alive and real.

A Sensory Experience with the Prophets

While pursuing a master's degree in creative writing, I undertook an independent study in modern poetry with a Jewish professor. We discussed the Bible quite often, particularly the prophets. So when she assigned me to write a poem in the persona of an Old Testament character, I chose the prophet Jeremiah, someone we'd often talked about. And in doing so I had a sensory experience that changed the way I viewed him.

I wrote the following poem in a voice I thought he might use in speaking to our modern culture:

jeremiah lives
ginsberg   howled   at the moon
while i   was knit   in the womb,
his thin, needle wail
a clanging   cymbal
in the night.

oh,
no voice speaks for him
no voice at all

i too have seen the best minds
of the generation:

camelot
drowned
in chappaquiddick,
a scurry, a flurry
in laos, l.a.,
memphis,

four dead
in o hi o.

truth! we cried

until the
tapes told
the truth of truth;

&
plunged us headlong
into saks or gucci
or civilized pan,

minked zen never curing

the war
in our hearts,

never hiding
naked fear.

today,
the women
still
come and go,

hating michelangelo

while blood itself could
fire-hose the street,

neither black nor white nor jew nor greek
is joined, fused

by speeches, rallies of
elite

oh my people

no voice
speaks for him

no voice
at all.

Joy Sawyer

While writing this poem I was surprised by many things, but one of the most revealing was how I came to feel about Jeremiah himself. Whenever I'd read his words before, I'd heard the voice of an angry madman, a man consumed with fury. But in the process of writing this poem in his voice, I was plunged into his emotional maelstrom, of which anger was only one whirling component. I also experienced a despondent, wailing, heartsick ache—the ache of the forgotten God, his feelings of deep betrayal and loss.

By using modern images I was familiar with—political situations and allusions to the work of Allen Ginsberg, Neil Young, T. S. Eliot— I could better imagine Jeremiah's pain: "You think you 'have seen the best minds of the generation'? All your great voices merely speak of your chaos, destruction, decay." I felt more deeply the anguish of Jeremiah as he saw God's eternal truth upstaged.

The overwhelming emotion of Jeremiah, as I experienced in writing this poem, was not anger but sorrow—grief and pain and the passionate desire to see the idols of false religion brought down and the true message of redemption proclaimed. I felt his fierce longing to penetrate my own soul's self-deception and to let God's Word dig even deeper into the hardest ground of my heart.

Foggy

Jeremiah shouts, "Break up
your fallow ground!" and as
I take my spade in hand, as far
as I can see, great clods of earth
are waiting, heavy and dark,
a hopeless task. First weeds will come,
then whatever it is
I've planted. I feel the struggle
in my knees and back.

All I can see
is close at hand,
monks who have
slouched, shuffled, stumbled, strutted,
and sauntered into church
this morning,

as they did yesterday,
and will again tomorrow.
Isn't that something? *I say*
to myself. I have no idea what,

except that it's happiness, pure
and simple, and questions fade
as great clouds
descend, as furrows
reel beneath my step: no what, *or* how, *or*
where is your God?
Only return, come back,
cleanse your hearts.

KATHLEEN NORRIS

Affected as Human Beings

The philosopher Paul Ricoeur says metaphor "gives rise to thought."[11] Ricoeur's "thought," however, doesn't just mean intellectual persuasion. As Frank Burch Brown elaborates, "Clearly the gift of metaphoric art lies not in rigorous and systematic argument but in its capacity to—in T. S. Eliot's words—'affect us wholly, as human beings.'"[12]

This was the poetic response of the apostle John toward Jesus: he was affected wholly, as a human being. In the opening of his first letter John doesn't offer an apologetic for Christ's miracles or teachings. Rather, he talks about how he and his friends had handled, held, seen, heard the person of Christ for themselves. John had had a sensory experience with the Metaphor: "From the very first day, we were there, taking it all in—we heard it with our own ears, saw it with our own eyes, verified it with our own hands. The Word of Life appeared right before our eyes; we saw it happen!" (1 John 1:1 *The Message*).

To Prove the Catch
(The Incredulity of St. Thomas, Caravaggio 1605)
Is having not seen really a blessing?
I'm envious of this filthy finger
Being guided, tracing glorified folds.
A fisherman probing, a baby bass mouth,
For his signature hook to prove the catch.

Is all that human dirt swimming around
Inside divine flesh, or do germs perish
On contact? Will the index be reborn
When he pulls out, or disappear, fused;
Left there to coagulate with God,

A link, to unbelieving men at watch?
Three bend; brows, freshly tilled by worried waiting,
Raw noses, reddened by the blood leftover,
From the Roman cellar where they last ate supper,
All eyes, sunken tearless wells, fixed in

Wonder, on this sacrament. I believe.
After a day's catch, the long vigil,
When scales and sweat have imbed callused pores
And clothes are ripped, from pulling through the waters,
This Bread, even with holes, looks heavenly.

KRISTY JOHNSON

The Plymouth Brethren writer C. A. Coates says that one of the marks of a true servant is that he is a witness first. And such a servant can only speak about what he has come to know for himself. Coates writes, "We may *minister* things which we have never entered into ourselves, but we cannot be *witnesses* of them." In the same way, both prophets and poets are, first and foremost, witnesses of what they've tasted, touched, handled for themselves.

Those who desire to live as prophetic metaphors are true servants—witnesses of life learned firsthand from God. Poetic witnesses don't ride the easy road of borrowing the popular ideas, beliefs and philosophies of others, as wonderful as those might be. Rather, they take the exhilarating trip of directly encountering the "heavenly Bread with holes" for themselves in the poetry workshop of the soul.

Our Prophetic Calling

Karl Shapiro writes, "What the poet sees with his always new vision is not what is 'imaginary'; he sees what others have forgotten to see."[13] The poet-prophet doesn't claim to present some new, dazzling truth. He or she simply shows us what we've already always known—and reminds us of it anew: "The revelation of truth that we get in the artist's work comes to us as a revelation of new truth . . . it is new, startling, and perhaps shattering—and yet it comes to us with a sense of familiarity. We did not know it before, but the moment the poet has shown it to us, we know that, somehow or other, we had always really known it."[14]

What we most need reminding of is not some complicated, twisting truth, but the simplest of all truths. That's why living poetically—and prophetically—isn't an esoteric exercise for the chosen few. It's about living out familiar truth.

A friend of ours recently told us this symbolic—yet true—story. He once served as the president of a Christian university, and during his tenure a bitter dispute erupted between the faculty and administration. Eventually the school did not renew the contracts of a handful of professors, and these same professors brought suit against the school.

For several years angry accusations were hurled back and forth between two distinct factions, those on the side of the university and those on the side of the professors. The local newspaper and television stations covered the dispute widely as the lawsuit moved into court. During the long, exhausting trial that followed, many people were hurt. Jobs were lost, long-time friendships discarded.

As all of this was happening, one of the faculty members who had initiated the lawsuit sent his résumé out to dozens of colleges, seeking work, only to be rejected time after time. Out of this dark crisis in his life, he began pursuing God in prayer as never before. And, over time, he developed a deep conviction that his decision to go to court against the university—his brothers and sisters in the faith—had been wrong.

While on his summer vacation, the former professor brought his family back to the city where the school was located, and he met with several of the university's faculty and administrators. He asked forgiveness of his former colleagues for his part in the legal battle. He wanted to clear his conscience before them, he said, and he was thankful they were willing to meet with him.

The faculty also asked him to forgive them, which he did. Then he left. Yet after the meeting, our friend, the university president, became convinced that something more was required of the situation.

He'd heard through another faculty member that the professor and his family were staying at a local YMCA. So, dressed in their dark business suits (as my friend jokingly described the group, "the Christian Men in Black"), he and two colleagues trekked through three separate YMCAs before they finally found the professor and his family splashing around in the pool.

As the three men strode purposefully toward them, the professor caught sight of them. He called their names, waved and climbed out of the pool to greet them. His wife watched uneasily from the water with their children.

As my friend approached, he held out his arms to the professor. Then he spoke.

"Jeff," he said, "we would like to invite you back to our university. You are too valuable of a professor and a Christian to lose. Will you rejoin us?"

The professor couldn't believe his ears. Immediately he loudly thanked God and hugged my friend. When his family saw this, they climbed out of the swimming pool, weeping and laughing, and embraced the other faculty members as well. After several minutes of this, my friend, soaking wet in his business suit alongside his colleagues, joked to the professor that he now had cause to fire him. At that point, a rollicking reunion took place.

The people lounging nearby in the striped beach chairs at the YMCA that day saw a bizarre vision: three men dressed in dark business suits embracing a wet, dripping family—all shedding tears of relief and forgiveness. My friend is no longer the president of that university, but he believes he was allowed the privilege of his office for that one, simple, chlorine-soaked moment.

It was also a prophetic moment.

Here's why: as Walter Brueggeman says, the prophet's task is to dismantle idolatry. It is to tear down anything that stands in the way of the words of God, so that those words are once again held supreme: "The exposure of Baalism as gods who cannot give life is equivalent to nullifying the political, cultural authority of the regime. Prophetic theology concerns the unmasking of the idols that keep the system functioning. Prophetic ministry has these exposures to make. There are false claimants to power who must be delegitimated in order that the true God have a say."[15]

How does the true God "have his say" today? As these university professors experienced, the unmasking of the idols in our souls comes through the simplest of actions.

In the poetry workshop of the soul, our lives are based on a new prophetic theology—the power of love and grace. And the words and life of Christ stand prophetically against systems, beliefs and authorities that illegitimately present themselves as his. I believe these men "nullified the political, cultural authority of the regime"—the regime of false religion—by offering mercy to one another. They brought down the Baal of bitterness and replaced it with Christ's forgiveness.

Throughout the New Testament our prophetic calling is made clear: believe Christ's words. Follow his life. Trust his heart. Listen to his voice. Yet sometimes these simplest truths, which require the simplest of actions, are the most difficult—and terrifying—to live out. As Oswald Chambers says, "It takes all God's power in me to do the most commonplace things in his way."

Like the prophets of old, the symbols we offer our culture are strange ones indeed—almost as strange as Jeremiah lying on his side in the middle of a busy street and tossing cow dung into the air. Consider: Protecting and paying respect to the weak, despised members of our community, because they're to be honored more than the strong, the wise, the powerful. Greatness that occurs not by climbing our way to the top of the bureaucratic heap but by burying ourselves as secret servants underneath it, looking for those dying in the suffocating shuffle. Forgiveness that extends itself to our offenders at least 490 times.

In the poetry workshop of the soul, the idols of our own selfish self-preservation can be dismantled by the selfless life of Jesus. Because of him and the work of his Spirit, we have the humbling, prophetic opportunity to beat our self-serving swords into the symbolic plowshares of his peace. To see the purple wine stains of our sins turned into living water.

Even YMCA swimming pool water.

Nine

Enjoying Beauty's Tension
The Paradox of Pleasure

*Poetry comes when the utmost reality
and the utmost strangeness coincide.*

JAMES DICKEY

The writer Dan Wakefield tells an interesting story about Mark Van Doren, the well-loved literature professor at Columbia University. As an undergraduate at Columbia, Wakefield took a class that Van Doren taught called "The Narrative Art." In it the students read classic literature—Homer, the Bible, Kafka. As Wakefield relates:

> On the last day of class, Van Doren asked us why we thought we had read those particular books. Being Columbia undergraduates, we all came up with these incredibly erudite, complicated answers. He would listen to each one of us and say, "Very interesting. But no, that's not it."
>
> Finally, with one minute to go on the clock, he said, "Gentlemen, the reason we read these books is that these are my favorite books." Then he walked out.[1]

Mark Van Doren (1946)

You know, he didn't teach me any thing;
The Chaucer, Edmund Spenser, Dante—wait!
I'm often etched by what he said of trimmers
(or by what he said that Dante said of them)
that they weren't wanted, even down in hell—
but otherwise (and that's the wise he was).
he taught me not a thing that I've remembered.

Why, then, is he the uppermost in mind
when I am asked—most often by myself—
"Who was the finest teacher you have known?"
The style, the style's the trick that keeps him kept—
no, not a trick; it must unfold as grace,
inevitably, necessarily,
as tomcats stretch, as sparrows scrounge for lice:
in such a way he lolled upon his desk
and fell in love before our very eyes
again, again—how many times again!—
with Dante, Chaucer, Shakespeare, Milton's Satan,
as if his shameless, glad, compelling love
were all that he really wanted us to learn;
no, that's not right; we were occasionals
who lucked or stumbled or were pushed on him—
he fell in love because he fell in love;
we were but windfall parties to those falls.

JAMES WORLEY

As this poet says so beautifully, he can't recall anything Mark Van Doren taught him. But what he does remember is that Van Doren *loved* what he taught him. The teacher's delight in Dante, Chaucer, Shakespeare ignited his students' souls. And years later that burning love for literature is what this poet carries with him.

Van Doren's deep, satisfying enjoyment of his serious, academic subject is a paradox. These most important things, he said in essence, are ultimately to be relished, to be savored. And the same thing seems true in God's creative process of spiritual growth: the paradox for every soul poet enrolled is that *we're invited to enjoy God before we serve him.* Grace offers us the gift of reveling in our Poet with a shameless, glad, compelling enjoyment, the way Van Doren did with literature.

Our spiritual journey in the poetry workshop of the soul begins with a supreme surprise. Instead of beginning by working toward fruitfulness, we're invited to relish our relationship with God—to feast, to drink. The awe-filled work of grace is that we give out of our appreciation for a remarkable heart gift we could never possibly earn.

Ironically this first work is difficult to do. It's Christmas day in our souls, but we're afraid to unwrap the huge, shiny red-and-green present. George Herbert captures the paradox of this struggle beautifully in his poem "Love (III)":

Love bade me welcome: yet my soul drew back,
  Guilty of dust and sin.
But quick-ey'd Love, observing me grow slack
  From my first entrance in,
Drew nearer to me, sweetly questioning,
  If I lack'd anything.

A guest, I answer'd, worthy to be here:
  Love said, You shall be he.
I the unkind, ungrateful? Ah my dear,
  I cannot look on thee.
Love took my hand, and smiling did reply,
  Who made the eyes but I?
Truth Lord, but I have marr'd them: let my shame
  Go where it doth deserve.
And know you not, says Love, who bore the blame?
  My dear, then I will serve.

You must sit down, says Love, and taste my meat:
   So I did sit and eat.

In the poem the narrator tells Love (God) every reason why he doesn't deserve grace. Finally he is struck by the paradoxical recognition of what Love offers him, and his immediate response is to want to serve. Love, however, has a different idea: your work is merely to sit down and eat, he says tenderly. Please, be my guest. Keep the feast.

Herbert's poem offers us a colorful prism through which to view the biblical story of the transfiguration (Mk 9:2-13). When Peter sees Jesus aglow in glory alongside Moses and Elijah in a supremely awe-inspiring moment, his first thought is to get to work in honor of the revelatory incident. He tells Jesus he wants to build shelters for all three. God's response? A voice from a cloud that simply says, "This is my Son, whom I love." You don't have to go to work, Peter. Just know that in this very moment I am delighting in my Boy. And that is enough for me.

Here is a most mysterious truth of our faith: even though Christ himself suffered deeply on our behalf, when he calls us to himself, he invites us to taste joy. The ultimate paradox is that, before we can serve, we're invited to be served by the Lord himself. "We love," says the apostle John, "because he first loved us" (1 Jn 4:19). And as Herbert's poem says so eloquently, the first service we offer God is to taste the grace he freely offers us. Only then can we offer it to others.

"Mostly what God does is love you," says Paul. "Keep company with him and learn a life of love. Observe how Christ loved us" (Eph 5:1 *The Message*).

These are all truths we think we want to hear. Who wouldn't? Yet, surprisingly, it also can chafe at our pride. We struggle as Peter did, resisting this "free" love: "No, Jesus, you will not wash my feet. I couldn't possibly allow you to do that." Yet it's Christ's very love—and the *joy* we have in receiving his love—that transforms us.

Dylan Thomas's poetry was marked forever by this same kind of surprising love. He said the reason he started writing poetry was because he fell in love with words. And he continued his artistic calling out of sheer delight. "I do not read poetry for anything but pleasure," he said. "And I read only the poems I like." He even declared that the joy and function of poetry was a celebration of God.[2]

March Morning

The diamond-ice-air is ribbon-laced
with brightness. Peaking wafering snowbanks are
sun-buttery, stroked by the
rosy fingertips of young
tree shadows
as if for music;
and all the eyes of God glow, listening.
> *My heart branches,*
> *swells into bud and spray;*
> *heart break.*

The neighbour's kid
lets fall his mitts
shrugs jacket loose
and wondering looks breathing the
crocus-fresh breadwarm
> *Being—*
easy as breathing.

Margaret Avison

The Pleasure of the Paradoxical Party

In the poetry workshop of the soul, the paradox of entering into God's pleasure and joy is a mind- (and heart-) altering mystery. Surprisingly, many of us prefer the certainty and finality of a funeral to the wild abandon and uncontrollable spirit of a wedding reception. We'd rather remain firmly in control, working our way to God, than *enjoy* him when we can—or allow him to enjoy us.

Yet like George Herbert, once we've experienced our need for forgiveness, we're beckoned to enter into the paradox of the full-hued, rainbow party of the joy of grace. We can unashamedly allow God to decorate our souls with his colorful confetti and silver Mylar balloons. We can leap off the cold, metal folding chairs of our works alone and rhumba at the dance party of redemption.

God's poetic paradox of grace invites us to fully experience the pleasures in our lives, to richly enjoy what brings us joy. It means we're free to live happily in the moment.

Every spring, I love when my bright-red tulips erupt from the brown earth. (This year, for the first time, there were yellow ones along with the red.) I love browsing with my husband for hours on end at our wonderful bookstore in Denver, The Tattered Cover, filled with the pungent smell of new covers and leather chairs.

Others tell me of their simple or obscure pleasures: listening to Mozart and Bach, or Sheryl Crow and Natalie Merchant. Progressive potlucks with friends. The fragrance of freshly mown grass. Watching foreign films. Hiking in the mountains and plunging their hands in rushing, icy streams. Sewing curtains and needlepointing pillows for friends. Lifting weights.

In those moments—and so many others—we experience tangible tastes of goodness. We savor redemption in the simple blessings of life, love, nature, friends, family. But our pleasurable moments also raise puzzling questions: Is God still good when we experience not joy but pain? After all, no matter what goodness we might experience in this life, we still tread the hard ground of a world that confronts us continually with confusion and heartache.

Another paradox arises then: How do we fully experience both pleasure and sorrow, even at the same time? How do we fully embrace our pain while still celebrating our blessings?

Tension Creates Beauty
Good poetry is often characterized by a paradoxical maxim: tension

creates beauty. The juxtaposition of unlike things squeezed together can produce gorgeous, moving art. In fact, one of the delights of writing a poem and watching it gracefully unfold is seeing how entirely unrelated things begin to weave together seamlessly.

In the poetry workshop of the soul, we're invited to enter such a "tension of unlike things"—to open our eyes and to see paradoxes in our lives, in the lives of others and in our faith. The life of Jesus is the best example of paradoxical mystery: "who for the sake of the *joy* that was set before him endured the cross" (Heb 12:2, emphasis mine). It's hard for us to imagine such joy. We know, for example, that Christ cried in the midst of his agony, "Father, why has thou forsaken me?" Yet the poetic paradox is that, along with his suffering, Jesus also experienced great *pleasure* in doing the will of the Father.

In his small, excellent book *Theopoetics,* theologian Amos Wilder discusses the term *Kreuzseligkeit,* or "blessedness in the cross." He says the term suggests that "Christian celebration is deepened by suffering and the early church's *hilarotēs* (hilarity) is possible without irresponsibility." Wilder's is no cynical, masochistic view of suffering. Rather, he invites us into paradox, because he recognizes "the believer's participation in that divine operation in which ultimate evil is encountered and transmuted."[3]

"The reaction of an audience to good poetry," says Karl Shapiro, "is laughter. . . . In fact, the basic emotion aroused by any work of art, however somber or tragic, is joy, even hilarity."[4]

Likewise, as we grow spiritually, we're invited to taste moments of joy—a sense of Wilder's blessedness—in the midst of sorrow. In this way we're entering into the poetic tension of beauty.

No matter what suffering or hardship awaits us in this life, we are headed toward hilarity—another home where God has triumphed forever over darkness. Our response to Christ's stunning poetry is to hold fast to his example of "for the joy set before him," that is, to eagerly look forward to that day. It is also glimpsing—and savoring—the tiny splinters of that glory in the now, even during our darkest moments.

"Rejoice always," urges Paul, who knew fully the dual experience of joy and pain. He knew that to embrace the paradox of the Christian life is to enter not only inevitable sufferings but also the strange hilarity of celebrating all things good and holy, both sorrowful and pleasurable. Yet, like Christ, Paul had no sentimental, naive view of delight. His was a deliberate recognition of the cost of following God. He knew the experience, both joyful and painful, of heeding Christ's words "I have said these things to you so that my joy may be in you, and that your joy may be complete" (Jn 15:11).

One Christmas a friend of ours, Al, sent us a story about his two-year-old son, Hunter. Al explained that one night, as their family returned from an outing, he and his wife, Nita, became deeply engrossed in a serious conversation about some difficult circumstances in their lives. A dark silence fell.

Suddenly they both heard Hunter in the back seat of the car, murmuring something. They listened more closely. "Beautiful," he said. Then again the same word, "Beautiful." Al and Nita looked at each other. Their son had never used the word before. Yet each time they drove past a lighted tree or house, Hunter looked out the window and whispered, "Beautiful."

Instead of going home, Al drove to a part of town where the trees were filled with thousands of bright, white lights. In the midst of their difficulties, he said, they took time to see and to enjoy. And they joined their son in his chorus.

Beautiful, they sang.

And experienced a tiny taste of kingdom paradox: surprising light in the midst of darkness.

Of consolation

It is down
makes
up seem
taller
black

sharpens white
flight
firms earth
underfoot
labor
blesses birth
with
later sleep

After silence
each sound
sings
dull clay
shines the
bright coin
in the pot
lemon
honeys its
sweet sequel
and my dark
distress
shows comfort
to be doubly
heaven-sent

LUCI SHAW

Living in a State of Paradox

Sometimes the most difficult work in the poetry workshop of the soul is to live in this perpetual state of paradox. In the Gospels Jesus always keeps us off balance. Just when we're ready to firmly state that Christ's chosen method is to preach and heal in front of thousands, he goes off and huddles with his friends on a secluded retreat. Then, just as we're about to exalt simplicity and quiet works, Jesus not only speaks to a crowd of five thousand but he feeds them lunch as well. As Herbert's poem says so vividly, it's when we're eager to go on ascetic duty for the cause that God invites us to sit down and savor pheasant under glass.

This is exactly what the apostle Peter experiences in Acts 10. Ready to meet his Lord in the holy mode of prayer, Peter instead receives a paradoxical vision of suddenly being commanded to eat a wide assortment of previously banned foods. We're talking about very definite, direct, in-the-moment, off-kilter leading—his own divine dining experience.

If we could only pin this God character to the wall, we'd be able to come up with a foolproof plan for our lives. We could confidently say that God's will is always that we build our huge cathedrals or stage our mass crusades or live quiet, contemplative lives—instead of constantly having to heart-lurch and head-spin into the fact that, at any given time, the Lord of surprises is up to something different. In the poetry workshop of the soul, we're invited to listen to God's Spirit, willing to be guided moment to moment by his gentle nudges and eye-opening revelations, whatever his choice may be.

The writer Annie Dillard advises us to wear crash helmets to church because God is a madman. He is not a domesticated puppy, cornered and corralled under our control. He is the wild-maned Lion of Judah, untamable, unchainable. And as Amos Wilder says, the "blessedness in the cross" he grants his followers, no matter what their circumstance or calling, is immeasurable.

Woolly, holy wonder roars around every corner—and we're on a life-long spiritual safari.

Peter's life may be the ultimate down-and-dirty example of the paradox of God. One would think that after the disciple's humiliating debacle of denial with the servant girl in the courtyard, he might spend several years licking his pride wounds and doing severe penance. Instead, Christ takes Peter—the most cowardly of the bunch—and, infusing him with his Spirit, props him up as his church's spokesperson on the Day of Pentecost.

Peter's story opens our eyes to an amazing truth: wherever God's Spirit is, there is the possibility of divine paradox. Thus, to live by paradox is to possess eyes and ears attuned to see and hear the startling, apparent incongruity of God's ways. It means finding ourselves curious about the Story beneath the story—lifting our heads to watch expectantly for the soaring flight of the divine that dances above our earthbound circumstances.

good friday
what?
anything but—

goodness stretched tight,
flesh-kite crookedly
snagged
between two branches.

horror descends, rends

history & hearts

in one moment
silent as loosened string:

mercy & madness meet,
dip, dance above us all.

& we,
seamed,
oblivious to spring
shrug off paradox,
a useless garment;

squat low & naked,
preferring the feel of flesh
to flight—

eyes dully fixed on

casting our lots

upon some
common ground.

JOY SAWYER

The Paradox of Humility

The paradox of humility is much like the story of the widow's mite in Mark 12, when a poor woman gave God all the money she had. Jesus and his disciples were at the temple, observing all the rich people who were making donations. Then they saw this tiny woman walk up and drop in her even tinier gift. When Jesus saw this, he turned to his followers and said, "Truly I tell you, this poor widow has put in more than all those who are contributing to the treasury. For all of them have contributed out of their abundance; but she out of her poverty has put in everything she had, all she had to live on" (Mk 12:43-44).

Even though this story is obviously about money, we can also connect it with other matters of poverty and abundance. As it was with the widow's mite, so it is with our hearts. Many begin their faith journey severely soul-impoverished. Yet as the widow's story tells us, we're never measured in terms of how outwardly big or small our gifts are, but by how much of our heart we pour out to God. Perhaps this is why Jesus cautions us so often not to judge others and instead to judge ourselves. The roughest person we know may allow God fuller reign in his soul than the most respected among us.

I once visited the church of an actress friend—a woman who left show business for a period of time to raise her young son. My friend is a passionate, colorful character, full of life and natural charisma. She is also a strongly committed Christian. Yet she struggled to fit within her church's culture. When she eventually returned to show business, she was immediately deemed prideful and unspiritual because of her profession.

One day she and I had coffee together. After she left, I felt a poem coming on. As I lagged behind in the greasy coffee joint, meditating on our conversation, I started to write. The last few lines of my scribbling read:

sometimes,
friend,
sometimes
in a world of night,
your greatest act of love—
your towel, your bowl—
is to humbly kneel
in all your splendor
& to burn
bright.

The poem led me on a new spiritual journey even as I wrote it: Humility isn't based on appearance, on assigning the label of "servanthood" to certain lowly tasks such as emptying trash cans or doing missions work. Humility is the honest enjoyment—and extravagant giving—of all the gifts we've been given in order to glorify God and to love others. The poem led me to the truth that humility isn't measured by what we do; it's in the heart behind what we do.

Because of the poem, I saw through new eyes the world of night that exists not only outside the church but inside it. And I saw how deeply we needed to see the fierce, burning light of Christ within this woman. That could only happen, however, if she remained entirely herself, contributing to the work of the body of Christ by enjoying and using all the splendid gifts she'd been given.

One night several months later, a small group of friends gathered at our apartment, including our actress friend. In the midst of a serious group discussion, our friend burst spontaneously into a Chekhov monologue—a piece that spoke directly to the personal issues we all

were facing. Her joy in performing his beautiful words—just for us—
deeply encouraged our faith.

That night our friend had brought her towel and bowl with her
and lovingly washed our calloused souls. Yet it was the very same
towel and bowl she brought with her when she performed on Broadway months later.

Both times we enjoyed a true servant burning brightly in paradoxical humility.

Poets of Paradox

To be a soul poet of paradox is to live happily amid startling oppo-
sites that are squeezed together into one. It means finding joy and
meaning in things that appear to be incongruent. The symbol of the
cross is, in itself, a paradox: the horizontal and the vertical nailed
together, our humanity and his divinity. Cross purposes serving a
greater purpose.

Whenever we flee paradox, we run from what is most holy in the
world, for the kingdom of God centers upon its puzzling poetry:
Jesus says the last shall be first. The greatest shall be the servant of
all. It is better to give than to receive. Bless those who curse you.
Pray for those who spitefully use you. Rejoice when others malign
you. Unless a seed falls into the earth and dies, it will never bear fruit.
Pray in secret and you will be rewarded openly.

Dylan Thomas remarks that the best poem "always leaves holes
and gaps in the works of the poem so that something that is *not* in
the poem can creep, crawl, flash, or thunder in."[5] Likewise the best
life poems always leave gaps for God to creep, crawl, flash and thunder through. And the life that dances to the heartbeat of redemption
will unashamedly reveal—even revel in—that surprising paradox:
God's resurrection power alive in human, struggling flesh.

As James Dickey says, poetry—and the poetry of the soul—is
when the utmost reality and the utmost strangeness coincide.

Opening

Now is the shining fabric of our day
Torn open, flung apart, rent wide by love.
Never again the tight, enclosing sky,
The blue bowl or the star-illumined tent.
We are laid open to infinity
For Easter love has burst His tomb and ours.
Now nothing shelters us from God's desire—
Not flesh, not sky, not stars, not even sin.
Now glory waits so He can enter in.
Now does the dance begin.

Elizabeth Rooney

Notes

Chapter 1: Living by Poetry
[1] e. e. cummings, *six nonlectures* (New York: Atheneum, 1972), p. 24.

[2] Karl Shapiro, "What Is Not Poetry?" in *The Poet's Work: 29 Masters of 20th Century Poetry on the Origins and Practice of Their Art*, ed. Reginald Gibbons (Boston: Houghton Mifflin, 1979), p. 100.

[3] Esther De Waal, *The Celtic Way of Prayer: The Recovery of Religious Imagination* (New York: Doubleday, 1997), p. 2.

[4] Ibid., pp. 2-3.

[5] Leland Ryken, *The Christian Imagination: Essays on Literature and the Arts* (Grand Rapids, Mich.: Baker, 1981), p. 263.

[6] D. Martyn Lloyd-Jones, *God's Way of Reconciliation: Studies in Ephesians 2* (Grand Rapids, Mich.: Baker, 1972), pp. 142-43.

[7] Arthur Lerner, ed., *Poetry as Healer: Mending the Troubled Mind* (New York: Vanguard, 1994), p. xi.

[8] Ryken, *Christian Imagination*, p. 270.

[9] Ibid.

[10] Ibid.

Chapter 2: Dancing to the Heartbeat of Redemption
[1] Richard Eberhart, *Of Poetry and Poets* (Urbana: University of Illinois Press, 1979), p. 35.

[2] James Reeves, *Understanding Poetry* (New York: Barnes & Noble, 1965), p. 33.

[3] Gabriel Marcel, *Being and Having* (Boston: Beacon, 1951), pp. 27-28.

[4] Rudolf Otto, *The Idea of the Holy*, trans. James W. Harvey (London: Oxford University Press, 1958), pp. xvi-xvii.

[5] Ibid.

[6] David Damrosch, "Leviticus," in *Literary Guide to the Bible*, ed. Robert Alter and Frank Kermode (Cambridge, Mass.: Belknap, 1987), p. 67.

[7] Donald Capps, *The Poet's Gift* (Louisville, Ky.: Westminster John Knox, 1993), pp. 1-2.

[8] Karl Shapiro, "What Is Not Poetry?" in *The Poet's Work: 29 Masters of 20th Century Poetry on the Origins and Practice of Their Art*, ed. Reginald Gibbons (Boston: Houghton Mifflin, 1979), p. 99.

[9] Donald Whittle, *Christianity and the Arts* (Oxford: Mowbray, 1966), p. 94.

[10] Shapiro, "What Is Not Poetry?" p. 100.

[11] Richard Wilbur, "Poetry and Happiness," in *Claims for Poetry*, ed. Donald Hall (Ann Arbor: University of Michigan Press, 1982), p. 473.

[12] Shapiro, "What Is Not Poetry?" p. 100.

[13] David Houston, "Defining Ourselves," *The Open Door* 54, no. 11 (November 1998): 5.

[14]Lawrence Sasek, *The Literary Temper of the English Puritans* (New York: Greenwood, 1961), p. 74.

Chapter 3: Conformed to the Image of Love
[1]William Packard, *The Art of Poetry Writing: A Guide for Poets, Students, and Readers* (New York: St. Martin's, 1992), p. 31.

[2]Ibid., pp. 31-32.

[3]James A. W. Heffernan, *Museum of Words: The Poetics of Ekphrasis from Homer to Ashbery* (Chicago: University of Chicago Press, 1993), pp. 1-3.

[4]Ibid.

[5]Ibid.

[6]Robert Bly, "What the Image Can Do," in *Claims for Poetry*, ed. Donald Hall (Ann Arbor: University of Michigan Press, 1982), p. 43.

[7]Dorothy Sayers, *The Mind of the Maker* (San Francisco: HarperSanFrancisco, 1987), p. 129.

[8]Diane Wakoski, in *The Poet's Craft: Interviews from the New York Quarterly*, ed. William Packard (New York: Paragon, 1987), p. 202.

[9]Luis Cernuda, "Words Before a Reading," in *The Poet's Work: 29 Masters of 20th Century Poetry on the Origins and Practice of Their Art*, ed. Reginald Gibbons (Boston: Houghton Mifflin, 1979), p. 43.

[10]Babette Deutsch, *Poetry in Our Time* (Garden City, N.Y.: Doubleday, 1963), p. 120.

[11]Donald Whittle, *Christianity and the Arts* (Oxford: Mowbray, 1966), p. 95.

[12]Chana Bloch, *Spelling the Word: George Herbert and the Bible* (Berkeley: University of California Press, 1984), p. 164.

Chapter 4: When Our Soul Sings the Blues
[1]Michael Ryan, "On the Nature of Poetry," in *Claims for Poetry*, ed. Donald Hall (Ann Arbor: University of Michigan Press, 1982), p. 365.

[2]William Packard, *The Art of Poetry Writing: A Guide for Poets, Students, and Readers* (New York: St. Martin's, 1992), pp. 35-36.

[3]Ryan, "Nature of Poetry," p. 365.

[4]Paul Fussell, *Poetic Meter & Poetic Form*, rev. ed. (New York: Random, 1979), p. 105.

[5]Ryan, "Nature of Poetry," p. 365.

[6]Denise Levertov, *New and Selected Essays* (New York: New Directions, 1992), p. 148.

[7]Andrew Lester, *Hope in Pastoral Care and Counseling* (Louisville, Ky.: Westminster John Knox), p. 89.

[8]Ibid., p. 22.

[9]Theodore Roethke, *On the Poet and His Craft*, ed. Ralph J. Mills Jr. (Seattle: University of Washington Press, 1965), p. 80.

[10]Ibid., p. 41.

[11]Brent Short, "A Figure for the Ghost: An Interview with Scott Cairns," *Mars Hill Review* 6 (fall 1996): 142.

[12]Karl Shapiro, "What Is Not Poetry?" in *The Poet's Work: 29 Masters of 20th Century Poetry on the Origins and Practice of Their Art*, ed. Reginald Gibbons (Boston: Houghton Mifflin, 1979), p. 102.

[13]Ibid., p. 85.

[14]Caroline Simon, *The Disciplined Heart: Love, Destiny & Imagination* (Grand Rapids, Mich.: Eerdmans, 1997), p. 89.

[15]Lester, *Hope in Pastoral Care*, p. 66.

[16]Ibid., p. 87.

Chapter 5: Developing the Poetic Voice

[1]William Packard, *The Art of Poetry Writing: A Guide for Poets, Students, and Readers* (New York: St. Martin's, 1992), p. 47.

[2]Arthur Lerner, "Poetry Therapy Corner," *Journal of Poetry Therapy* 11, no. 3 (spring 1998): 183.

[3]Rainer Maria Rilke, *Letters to a Young Poet* (New York: W. W. Norton, 1934), p. 18.

[4]For more information on Precious Oil Ministries, an outreach to the comatose and their families, contact John and Gail Wessells at P.O. Box 511, Otego, NY 13825, (607) 988-6535, or e-mail: PreciousJW@aol.com. The full story of Bob is included in Scott and Joy Sawyer, "True Awakenings," *Christianity Today*, March 8, 1993, pp. 16-19.

[5]John N. Wall Jr., ed., *George Herbert* (New York: Paulist, 1981), p. xiii.

[6]Joy Sawyer, "The Holy Hunger: Biblical Recreation in the Work of Gerard Manley Hopkins and George Herbert" (master's thesis, New York University, 1993).

[7]Chana Bloch, *Spelling the Word: George Herbert and the Bible* (Berkeley: University of California Press, 1984), pp. 1-2.

[8]Ibid., p. 172.

[9]Ibid., p. 45.

[10]Ibid., p. 91.

[11]Galway Kinnell, *Walking down the Stairs: Selections from Interviews* (Ann Arbor,: University of Michigan Press, 1978), p. 6.

[12]Theodore Roethke, *On the Poet and His Craft*, ed. Ralph J. Mills Jr. (Seattle: University of Washington Press, 1965), p. 42.

[13]Wendell Berry, "The Specialization of Poetry," in *The Poet's Work: 29 Masters of 20th Century Poetry on the Origins and Practice of Their Art*, ed. Reginald Gibbons (Boston: Houghton Mifflin, 1979), p. 143.

Chapter 6: Community as Soul Critics

[1]Galway Kinnell, *Walking down the Stairs: Selections from Interviews* (Ann Arbor, Mich.: University of Michigan Press, 1978), p. 76.

[2]T. S. Eliot, *The Sacred Wood* (London: Methuen, 1960), pp. 37-38.

[3]Ibid., p. 7.

[4]Marvin Bell, "The Impure Every Time," in *Claims for Poetry*, ed. Donald Hall (Ann Arbor: University of Michigan Press, 1982), p. 11.

[5]Mary Oliver, *A Poetry Handbook* (New York: Harcourt Brace, 1994), p. 116.

[6]William Carlos Williams, "Projective Verse," in *The Poet's Work: 29 Masters of 20th Century Poetry on the Origins and Practice of Their Art*, ed. Reginald Gibbons (Boston: Houghton Mifflin, 1979), p. 192.

[7]Ron Padgett, ed., *The Teachers & Writers Handbook of Poetic Forms* (New York: Teachers & Writers Collaborative, 1987), pp. 189-90.

[8]Ibid.

[9]Denise Levertov, *New and Selected Essays* (New York: New Directions, 1992), p. 78.

[10]Padgett, *Teachers & Writers Handbook*, p. 85.
[11]Paul Fussell, *Poetic Meter & Poetic Form*, rev. ed. (New York: Random House, 1979), p. 77.
[12]Ibid., p. 88.
[13]Padgett, *Teachers & Writers Handbook*, p. 89.
[14]Ibid., p. 91.
[15]Ibid.
[16]Ibid., pp. 98-99.
[17]Ibid., p. 65.
[18]Ibid.
[19]Ibid.
[20]Kinnell, *Walking down the Stairs*, p. 53.
[21]Hayden Carruth, "The Question of Poetic Form," in *Claims for Poetry*, ed. Donald Hall (Ann Arbor: University of Michigan Press, 1982), p. 57.
[22]John Macmurray, *Persons in Relation* (Atlantic Highlands, N.J.: Humanities Press, 1991), pp. 157-58.
[23]Leland Ryken, *The Christian Imagination: Essays on Literature and the Arts* (Grand Rapids, Mich.: Baker, 1981), p. 270.

Chapter 7: The Blessing of Brokenness

[1]William Carlos Williams, "Projective Verse," in *The Poet's Work: 29 Masters of 20th Century Poetry on the Origins and Practice of Their Art*, ed. Reginald Gibbons (Boston: Houghton Mifflin, 1979), pp. 196-97.
[2]Galway Kinnell, *Walking down the Stairs: Selections from Interviews* (Ann Arbor: University of Michigan Press, 1978), p. 14.
[3]Madeleine L'Engle, *Walking on Water* (Wheaton, Ill.: Harold Shaw, 1980), p. 99.
[4]Kathleen Norris, "Of Poets and Monks," *Christian Century*, July 27-August 3, 1994, p. 722.
[5]Rainer Maria Rilke, *Letters to a Young Poet* (New York: W. W. Norton, 1934), p. 68.
[6]Dorothy Sayers, "Toward a Christian Aesthetic," in *The New Orpheus: Essays Towards a Christian Poetic*, ed. Nathan Scott (Kansas City: Sheed & Ward, 1964), pp. 15-16.
[7]Robert Wilson, *Man Made Plain: The Poet in Contemporary Society* (Cleveland: Howard Allen, 1958), p. xiv.
[8]René Char, "From the Formal Share," in *The Poet's Work: 29 Masters of 20th Century Poetry on the Origins and Practice of Their Art*, ed. Reginald Gibbons (Boston: Houghton Mifflin, 1979), p. 63.
[9]Dietrich Bonhoeffer, *Prisoner for God: Letters and Papers from Prison* (New York: Macmillan, 1954), pp. 123-24.
[10]Richard Eberhart, *Of Poetry and Poets* (Urbana: University of Illinois Press, 1979), p. 81.

Chapter 8: Living as Sacred Symbols

[1]M. Dick, "Prophetic *Poiesis* and the Verbal Icon," *The Catholic Biblical Quarterly* 46 (1984): 228.
[2]Jan Wojcik and Raymond-Jean Frontain, eds., "Introduction: The Prophet in the Poem," in *Poetic Prophecy in Western Literature* (London: Associated University Presses), p. 28.

[3]Ibid., p. 17.

[4]Denise Levertov, *New and Selected Essays* (New York: New Directions, 1992), p. 148.

[5]Walter Brueggeman, *The Prophetic Imagination* (Philadelphia: Fortress, 1978), pp. 48-50.

[6]Sharon Gallagher, "On Imagination, Writing, and Worship: An Interview with Luci Shaw," *Radix* 22 (1994): 14.

[7]Delmore Schwartz, "The Vocation of the Poet in the Modern World," in *The Poet's Work: 29 Masters of 20th Century Poetry on the Origins and Practice of Their Art*, ed. Reginald Gibbons (Boston: Houghton Mifflin, 1979), p. 83.

[8]Ibid., p. 12.

[9]Denise Levertov, "An Admonition," in *Claims for Poetry*, ed. Donald Hall (Ann Arbor: University of Michigan Press, 1982), p. 253.

[10]Dana Gioia, *Can Poetry Matter? Essays on Poetry and American Culture* (St. Paul: Greywolf, 1992), p. 245.

[11]R. Hazelton, "Theological Analogy and Metaphor," *Semeia* 13 (1978): 161.

[12]Frank Burch Brown, "Transfiguration: Poetic Metaphor and Theological Reflection," *The Journal of Religion* 12 (1982): 48.

[13]Karl Shapiro, "What Is Not Poetry?" in *The Poet's Work: 29 Masters of 20th Century Poetry on the Origins and Practice of Their Art*, ed. Reginald Gibbons (Boston: Houghton Mifflin, 1979), p. 100.

[14]Dorothy Sayers, "Toward a Christian Aesthetic," in *The New Orpheus: Essays Towards a Christian Poetic*, ed. Nathan Scott (Kansas City: Sheed & Ward, 1964), pp. 15-16.

[15]Walter Brueggeman, "The Prophet as Destabilizing Presence," in *The Pastor as Prophet*, ed. Earl E. Shelp and Ronald H. Sunderland (New York: Pilgrim, 1985), p. 69.

Chapter 9: Enjoying Beauty's Tension

[1]Scott and Joy Sawyer, "A Great Circle Coming Fully Around: A Conversation with Dan Wakefield," *Mars Hill Review* 4 (winter-spring 1996): 104.

[2]Dylan Thomas, "Poetic Manifesto," in *The Poet's Work: 29 Masters of 20th Century Poetry on the Origins and Practice of Their Art*, ed. Reginald Gibbons (Boston: Houghton Mifflin, 1979), pp. 184-90.

[3]Amos Wilder, *Theopoetics: Theology and the Religious Imagination* (Philadelphia: Fortress, 1976), p. 11.

[4]Karl Shapiro, "What Is Not Poetry?" in *The Poet's Work: 29 Masters of 20th Century Poetry on the Origins and Practice of Their Art*, ed. Reginald Gibbons (Boston: Houghton Mifflin, 1979), p. 100.

[5]Thomas, "Poetic Manifesto," p. 190.